You there,

with your

glory-starved

heart and

your one

fleeting life,

I want you

to hear Me...

FINDING GOD
AT THE KITCHEN SINK

search for glory in the everyday grime

MAGGIE PAULUS

MOODY PUBLISHERS, CHICAGO

Maggie Paulus belongs to the society A. W. Tozer called "the fellowship of the burning heart." She's on a hunt—a hunt for beauty and rest, for the slaking of those longings and desires that linger deep down in every human soul. And in this gem of a book, she invites us to join the hunt, recounting along the way the brokenness of her past, the ordinariness of her present, and the glorious hope she has discovered in Jesus. C. S. Lewis wrote about finding patches of Godlight in the woods of our experience. Well, this beautiful book is full of Godlight. I hope you'll read it.

> —**BRIAN G. HEDGES**, pastor and author

Captivating! Every page breathes fresh gospel hope. Maggie masterfully weaves life-story with His story and then beckons us to imagine the extraordinary, almost unimaginable significance and mission that exists in the mundaneness of our daily realities. I laughed. I cried. And I was drawn to know Him more.

> —**CARRIE GAUL**, author, *Joy in the Midst: A Study in Philippians*

Maggie has a child's eyes, an artist's soul, and a lover's heart. Some books make wise. This book reveals the God who makes good. Grab your coffee, cookies, and Kleenex, and (as Maggie puts it) get ready for your Maker to "scribble round the edges of your heart."

> —**DEL FEHSENFELD III**, senior editor of *Revive* Magazine, Life Action Ministries

Maggie has been a longtime friend of our family, and I've always admired the way she notices beauty and the grace of God in both nature and the people around her. She takes the time, in her ordinary routine, to thank and praise God, and marvel at the work of His hand. That's a gift. In *Finding God at the Kitchen Sink*, Maggie shares that gift with us!

—**CARRIE WARD**, author, *Together: Growing Appetites for God*

With homespun style that won't let you go, Maggie lives and breathes God in every detail. She helps us appreciate that there is no humdrum when it comes to discovering God in the daily grind. Real struggles can become real strides forward with Maggie as a reliable guide.

—**BYRON PAULUS**, president, Life Action Ministries, Buchanan, MI

If we ever needed the reminder that God will meet us where we are in our messy, broken lives, this is it. Maggie beautifully shows us how to see God in the midst of our everyday lives— both in the exceptional and the mundane. A must-read for those desperate to recognize God's fingerprints on their life.

—**NATALIE LEDERHOUSE**, assistant editor, *Today's Christian Woman*

Thank you for affirming me and praying for me—when we wake up in the morning or on your lunch break and even in the middle of the dark night. Thank you for speaking words into my life that have helped and have healed. Thank you for choosing me. Over and over again. And thank you for being goofy and making me laugh more than anyone else in this big wide world. I dig all your groovy, uncoordinated dance moves. I love you.

AND FOR MY SWEET LOVES, GIDEON, HOPE, AND SAMUEL.

You've taught me so much about the kingdom, through your curious questions at the breakfast table and when I'm tucking you in your beds at night. I've loved seeing the world through your eyes, all full of wonder. You encourage me deep with your hope-filled belief in things you can't yet see. You began in God's heart—may He always be your true Home.

I'm so glad I get to be your momma.

© 2014 by
MAGGIE PAULUS

Edited by Bailey Utecht
Cover & Interior design: Erik M. Peterson
Cover photo of window sill copyright © 2014 by Maggie Paulus. All rights reserved.
Photographs © 2014 by Maggie Paulus. All rights reserved.
Author photo: Katie Bollinger

Library of Congress Cataloging-in-Publication Data

Paulus, Maggie.
  Finding God at the kitchen sink : search for glory in everyday grime / Maggie Paulus.
    pages cm
  ISBN 978-0-8024-1180-8
  1. Spirituality—Christianity—Meditations. 2. God (Christianity)—Omnipresence—Meditations.
3. Christian women—Religious life—Meditations. I. Title.
BV4501.3.P39 2014
248.4—dc23

                            2014008163

Moody Publishers is committed to caring wisely for God's creation
and uses recycled paper whenever possible. The paper in this book
consists of 10 percent post-consumer waste.

We hope you enjoy this book from Moody Publishers. Our goal is to provide high-quality,
thought-provoking books and products that connect truth to your real needs and challenges. For
more information on other books and products written and produced from a biblical perspective, go
to www.moodypublishers.com or write to:

Moody Publishers
820 N. LaSalle Boulevard
Chicago, IL 60610

1 3 5 7 9 10 8 6 4 2

Printed in the United States of America

A special thank you to
Erik M. Peterson for taking my own
pictures, these pieces of my life, and remarkably
crafting the cover and interior design. I'm so
glad God made artists. You're a good, <u>good</u> one.

A WORD
FROM MAGGIE

DEAR ONE,

I don't know where today finds you. Perhaps you're sitting by your window, there on one of the middle floors of the high-rise that looks out above all the city lights. And you've got your coffee and you've lit your candle and you're leaning on your pillow as the rain pelts gently on the glass, little rivulets streaming down all slow and quiet and steady.

Or perhaps you're there in the coffee shop, sitting next to strangers. You've got your book and you're settling in there in your seat, looking for some solace.

Or maybe you're a momma and you've finally got your peace because the kids just went to sleep, and there are still dishes and a heaping pile of laundry, but you're done for the night. You just curled up on the couch and you're way too tired to read, but you'd like to try anyway.

One thing I do know about you . . . this I know about all of us here—trying to find our way, scratching out a living on this pale-blue dot that spins, tilted and twirling through space. I know it doesn't matter if you're a highly intellectual atheist or a deeply devoted spiritual. It makes no difference if you've made it to the top of the corporate ladder or if you're one of those folks down at the grocery store who scrubs the commode. Because there is this one thing we all have in common, and it is this: we're all painfully broken—every last one of us—and it's our brokenness that brings us all together here, huddled in all collective and close.

So while we're huddled here, I'd like to tell you some stories, give you some glimpses into my heart. A piecing together of my days. Now, you should know, though, that these glimpses are a bit messy. That is, they come from a messy life. But isn't that all we really have to give each other—our tangled up stories from our complicated lives? And we really do need them, you and I. We need each other's muddled musings and twisted up thoughts because we've got to know that in all this struggle and strain, we're not alone. We were never meant to be alone. Our stories are the hands reaching out to take hold of each other when the ground beneath us trembles and the world around us quakes.

And as you read the scribbling down of my days, these bits and pieces of my one and only life, I hope you'll discover some things. There are some things I really want you to know.

I want you to know there is a God, a great Author who always ever was, who is weaving His story into our days. And if, by chance, life has turned you a bit cynical or jaded to any notion of a Maker, my hope is that your eyes would wake up wide to see His glory and your heart would beat wild with the whooshing, pulsing wonder of His grace.

And I hope you'll see this God doesn't live in boxes, nor is He confined to church houses or sacred assemblies. He dwells *here* with us in all the moments of our everyday, humdrum life.

I want you to feel in the deepest part of you that all your running-together days—though chock-full of common, ordinary, seemingly insignificant things—are not some erratic succession of events, a mere twenty-four hours in which you plod along and aimlessly exist. No, these days . . . each and every one of them is brimful of meaning and purpose. This new day *matters* because the God who conducts the wind and made the moss grow rampant beneath the maples, the One who fills up heaven, is ever present with you in your one, fleeting life. The One who calls Himself the Great *I AM* actually *is*. *Right here.*

And it's this God who has given you the beauty ache, that ravishing desire to find good in the mess, to hunt for glory in the grime. When you go looking for beauty and hunting for glory, you'll discover again and again the realness of Him: the God who is *there* and is not silent. The One who all the while— when you were grappling around in the dark, searching for His face, some notion of grace in a fallen, wrecked-up world—was there. Standing near and bending down close enough so the moment you reached up, barely stretching out with one speck of faith, you could take hold of Him.

Yes, I want you to know—you with your brokenness, your chaotic days, and your one, fleeting life—I want you to know there is a Maker who isn't far from each one of us. He very much wants to be found.

So I scribble down my stories for you. And I testify to this—
that I have seen God-glory. And now I can't help but live in
awe of the Eternal One who has woven His narrative into my
days.

I hope you see Him too.

PREFACE

I DON'T KNOW THE CIRCUMSTANCES, EXACTLY, OF my parents' lives when I first entered this world and their existence. I know they were painfully broken people. And though I was only a little thing the last time I saw them, I remember them quite well. The way my momma was gentle and easygoing when she was sober. I always wanted to sleep next to her on the occasional night she was home. I craved her close. So when she rolled over, I'd protest and beg her to turn herself back around because I felt more secure, her face right next to mine.

I remember my daddy and the way he carried me, sort of perched up there on his arm, all awkward-like, the way daddies carry children. I'd keep slipping and he'd keep boosting, but I didn't mind because I felt safe up close, my little hand curled around his neck. And when he stopped at the gas station for more beer and cigarettes, I'd beg for candy, and he always got me some. I suppose he was a softy like that.

My birth parents were kind to me, but they had hurts and they had addictions and they didn't know how to take care of themselves, much less a wee girl and her little brother.

They tried. They hung on to us the first five years of my life, but things kept slipping and they kept falling and failing. They mustered up what strength they could, but they couldn't make it work and they couldn't make it right. And so the policemen came, over and over again, and took me and my little brother away. And I remember how my momma cried in the back of the police car the last time the police caught up with us, her hands cuffed, and she told me she loved me. I knew in my little heart—as I looked up at her with her tears streaming and mascara running—I knew she did love me. She couldn't make it work.

And I can still recall my daddy's face another time when the police caught up with him, this worn-out, haunted look in his eyes. I watched through the car window and wondered how his hair got such a mess, my little legs not even long enough to dangle from the seat. They took his drugs and took his booze and took us kids. Even though I was a wee girl, I knew deep inside that he was in trouble and he couldn't make it right.

And I cried for them because every little girl wants her mommy and needs her daddy, but they were gone, *again*, and I felt lost. And the social workers took us to some foster homes, lots of times they took us, but we weren't all that safe. Sometimes bad guys live in foster homes and I lay in bed at night wishing they would go away. That was back when I was just a little thing.

But one day something surprising happened. Something strange. The social workers came to our foster home, put our stuff in a brown paper bag, and drove us to their office where we met a different mom and dad. And when we walked in, the two of them sat there, kind and smiling, beside the big, long table. They tried to explain that they wanted us. Like, forever. And we could live with them, and they'd be our family and never go away. The social workers asked us if we'd like that. And I liked the idea, but I didn't know what it actually meant to stay. I had learned not to trust the grown-ups, so deep inside I didn't quite believe. At least, not *yet*.

But sure enough, we went to our new home and I had a big brother and a big sister. They loved us from the get-go and never made us feel like we didn't belong. And my new mom and dad told me the story about how they had prayed for us because God had put us in their hearts, but they didn't know where to start or what to do. So they went through all the ropes and jumped through all the hoops, and they became the kind of parents who could adopt children from broken homes. The social workers gave them picture albums, lots and lots of picture albums, and told them to pick out some kids. So they sat, hopeful, and they searched through and ached for all these kids who God made. But they needed Him to make it crystal clear, so they flipped through those pages and asked in faith that He would point us out and help them see.

And one day my new momma walked into the government office, saw our picture on the desk, and knew right away. She told the social worker that we were *her* kids, because she recognized us. Sure enough, God had helped her see. And the lady looked at her all puzzled and said it wasn't true and it wasn't even possible, but Momma knew about the God of all the impossibles. So she didn't back down. She and Daddy recruited some friends and they all prayed. It wasn't long after that we came home. For good. And time passed and no one ever took us away. So I believed.

And as days have turned to months that have turned to years,

I still believe. I believe in a God of all the impossibles. And I've come to find He's the One who rescues and He redeems, but He uses our hands and our feet. And He whispers His rescue plan into our hearts and hopes we'll obey.

And this same God has healed my wounds from a momma and a daddy who couldn't make it work and couldn't make it right. He gave me another momma and daddy who didn't have it all together but who depended on the only One who does. And people say time heals all wounds, but I think it's love that does the healing.

And every day I'm thankful I've been rescued and my life has been redeemed by the God who can make beauty from a busted-up mess. And I'm thankful for a family who became His hands and feet to reach out with a love that heals—reached out to the likes of my brother and me. When I was a little thing.

> *Let them thank the Lord for his steadfast love,*
> *for his wondrous works to the children of man!*
> *And let them offer sacrifices of thanksgiving,*
> *and tell of his deeds in songs of joy!*
>
> PSALM 107:21–22

men, and they were fishing in the lake with a net. Jesus said, "Come follow me. I will make you fishermen for men." At once Simon and Andrew left their nets and followed him.

Jesus continued walking by Lake Galilee. There he saw two other brothers, James and John, the sons of Zebedee. They were in a boat with their father Zebedee, preparing their nets to go fishing. Jesus told them to come with him, and they left the boat and their father, and followed Jesus.

Jesus Teaches and Heals People

Jesus went everywhere in Galilee. He taught in the synagogues and preached the Good News about the kingdom of heaven. And he healed all the people's diseases and sicknesses. The news about Jesus spread all over

A QUIET COFFEE MORNING

I GET UP EARLY AND ENJOY A quiet, coffee morning because I miss God. Something in me wants to be with my Maker. I want to sit beside Him and hear His voice. So I open up His Word to Matthew 5 where Jesus teaches about life to this great big crowd of people, and I listen to Him talking.

He speaks.

> *Seeing the crowds, he went up on the mountain, and when he sat down, his disciples came to him.*
> MATTHEW 5:1

Just one verse. That's all I need for now. This is Jesus talking to me. His words nourish my heart, and I think about what

He means. *He saw the crowds . . .* when Jesus looked out into a crowd of people, He didn't *just* see a sea of faces. He saw each individual person standing there with all their soul-ache. He knew where each one had come from, all they'd been through, and He looked deep into every single heart. They could hide behind each other if they wanted, but they couldn't hide all their insides from Him. Not from the God who sees past all the skin into what makes us who we are.

Then I think about the crowd in my own heart. I mean, don't we all carry a crowd of people around in our heart? I look inside and I see a myriad of people who I love and pray for, and I carry them with me and wonder if God sees them. He does. He sees and knows—*intimately* knows—each heart and He aims to speak into their life.

I ponder more of His words. *He went up on the mountain . . . He sat down.* This God who made the mountains, now humble like us, was climbing up all the dirt and rocks so He could look out into all the faces. He sits down. God sits down. He's not too busy. He's not too rushed. He doesn't have too much to do. This is His important thing. To sit and speak words that help and heal whoever will sit still enough to listen. And all their lives these people had missed God. Something deep inside them had always wanted to be with Him and now here He was. So they sat a while and spent time with the One who could see past the facade right into all their brimming ache. They were hungry and His words fed them. They were soul-shattered and His words made them whole.

The disciples came to Him. Am not I His follower, too? So I come to Him on a quiet coffee morning and sit at His feet. Because I miss God and I want to be with Him. He's my Maker and He's also my friend.

And this Jesus, He still looks out across the world and sees the crowds of people. And in a sea of faces, He still knows the heart behind each one. He still sits and speaks words that nourish and bring life to whoever will stop long enough to listen.

> *"Be still, and know that I am God. I will be exalted among the nations, I will be exalted in the earth!" The Lord of hosts is with us; the God of Jacob is our fortress.*
>
> PSALM 46:10-11

WHAT GOD IS LIKE

SOMETIMES MY HUSBAND, BRENT, SCOOPS UP OUR daughter and cradles her on his lap. He gently lays Hope's little head down on his chest and holds her close . . . just because. Just because he's her daddy and she's his little girl.

And that's what God is like.

Sometimes Hope picks up her doll and takes her for a stroll. She wraps her little blanket around her and tucks in all the sides, just so. She feeds her and rocks her and gives her a kiss— smudgy cheeks and all—because she loves her baby doll.

And that's what God is like.

Sometimes my son Gideon notices when someone is sad. He knows what it feels like to have a hard time, and in his concern he wants to make it better. So he says things like, "Don't be sad. I'll take care of you." He means it with all his heart.

And that's what God is like.

When my littlest guy, Samuel, sees his brother or sister nearby, he squeals with a raucous delight. He's so happy they exist. And when their face is anywhere close to his, he reaches out, takes hold of their cheeks, and pulls them in.

And that's what God is like.

Sometimes in the night, I wake up and look over at Brent and enjoy him here with me. I lie quiet. I watch his chest rise and fall with each new breath. And I smile, thankful.

And oftentimes I get up to go peek at little ones asleep in their beds and marvel at the beauty of their faces, full of peace and rest. My heart fills up with delight and I love them immensely, because they're mine. I know without a doubt I'd lay down my life for my children.

And that's what God is like.

Anyone who does not love does not know God, because God is love.

1 JOHN 4:8

So we have come to know and to believe the love that God has for us. God is love, and whoever abides in love abides in God, and God abides in him.

1 JOHN 4:16

HUNGRY STILL

TODAY I WATCH THE SKY MOVE. TURBULENT clouds swirl and eddy across the marvelous deep above me. Something about it reminds me of the underside of a seashell. The way the ripples and whirls curve under and smooth out all fluid-like.

And when I look up at the sky, I think of big things. High things. Long things. Like eternity and never-ending life. I imagine one of those clouds peeling back so I can see through to the other side. To forever. To the God I can't stop longing for.

On this stormy July morning, I attest to this—I entered this world with a ravishing hunger. A yearning for something. Someone who will awe me. Undo me. Overwhelm me with His breathtaking beauty. And the purpose of this craving is to drive me to the Source of deepest satisfaction. To my chief delight. To *Him*. So I may know Him. Touch Him. Taste Him. Be filled up to the brim and overflowing with Him—Him in all His heart-stirring wonder.

And if I was made to be filled up with God, then it makes sense why everything else leaves me empty. I can never get enough of all the stuff of the world. Never enough clothes. Or money. *Things*. Never enough entertainment. Always needing something—one more possession that will surely make me happy at last. But I'm left disappointed because it's all so fleeting, so temporary. Like the one cloud already spreading thin. I can barely trace the outline. Like this earthly existence—this one life we've been given that we think is all there is. How quickly it passes, spreads thin, and then is gone.

So I lean forward. I take steps toward Him: to the One who one day these very eyes will see. My heart leaps when I think of the reality of this. And when I look over the horizon, I barely catch a glimpse. His kingdom light bleeding through, seeping into my here and now. I worship. And I am filled.

> *He has made everything beautiful in its time. Also, he has put eternity into man's heart.*
>
> ECCLESIASTES 3:11

My response is to get down on my knees before the Father, this magnificent Father who parcels out all heaven and earth. I ask him to strengthen you by his Spirit—not a brute strength but a glorious inner strength—that Christ will live in you as you open the door and invite him in. And I ask him that with both feet planted firmly on love, you'll be able to take in with all followers of Jesus the extravagant dimensions of Christ's love. Reach out and experience the breadth! Test its length! Plumb the depths! Rise to the heights! Live full lives, **full in the fullness of God.**

EPHESIANS 3:14–19 THE MESSAGE

WHEN YOU'RE
NOT EXACTLY
A SUPERHERO

GIDEON WAKES UP WAY TOO EARLY, AND I groan. I'm not mentally prepared yet for all the loud, and I was desperately hoping for some more quiet. Quiet to think. Quiet to pray. Quiet to read and meditate. Quiet to soak in God and let Him fill all my empty, aching places. But not this morning. Mr. Tasmanian was alert, alive, and enthusiastic. So I roll my eyes and brace myself for another rambunctious-boy-energy whirl of a day.

He can't help it. He's a curious little fella and he's got all these questions. I mean, he *needs* to know the life cycle of a corn stalk and where the milk truck *actually* goes after it leaves the barn, and where we're going after breakfast, and then what we're doing right after that. I repeat an awful lot of "I don't knows." We stir pink cream of wheat because he wants to color it red but instead it turns out pink. I look up at the clock and it's not even eight. I'm already worn out. This could be one of those grueling days.

Then he asks to go upstairs and pat Hope's back, which is actually code for, "I want to wake up Hope so she can play with me," which actually turns out to mean, "I don't want Hope to actually *play* with me, I want her to stand supportively next to me and cheer me on in all my endeavors." I refuse to let him go pat her back. He cries. I could cry, too.

The house is a wreck again and I have this hilarious mental picture of myself. Basically, I'm standing in the living room in some overly tight spandex, looking a lot like a superhero. Only I don't have any superpowers or any superhuman strength— just a hopeful disposition I could conquer this place with my vacuum and squirt bottle and my flapping cape. It helps, this mental picture, and I grin because I'm a superhero on the inside, making everything right again.

Brent hugs me before he leaves for work and prays for us and for this day, and I don't ask God for superpowers but for a new

heart . . . a *thankful* one. The cloud lifts. And I've still got my flailing shortcomings, but I remember that's the point of Jesus. His righteousness covering all my sins. Today is another gift, and when God sees me, He's looking out through the lens of His perfect Son, so I am pure and I'm spotless and it's like I'm new all over again. I don't need a lot of quiet time to remember that.

I can hear Gideon singing, "He's got the whoooole world, in His hands . . ." and I sing it, too. He's got me. Always got me. And He's got all this world, including all the mess. And He's making something good again today. So I take one step at a time, breathe in grace and exhale thanks. All this noise becomes a joyful melody and all this commotion a dance. Thankfulness. It *is* good medicine.

> *Do all things without grumbling or disputing, that you*
> *may be blameless and innocent, children of God without*
> *blemish in the midst of a crooked and twisted generation,*
> *among whom you shine as lights in the world.*
> PHILIPPIANS 2:14–15

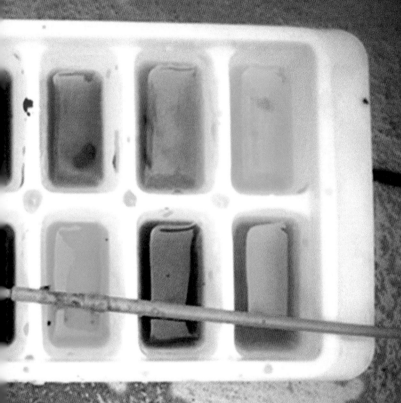

God is here. Just right *here*.

THE SHOUT-OUT

I heard it today. The shout-out. The way God says *I love you*.

I heard it in the morning, when a group of friends came trampling through my front door bringing powdered donuts and orange juice and gifts for our newborn babe, Samuel.

Again I heard it at noon: kids giggling on the living-room floor building block towers and pillow castles and marching around the couch with their clashing symbols and harmonica songs.

And in the evening, I heard it. Loud and clear. The shout. The *I love you* shout. God sang it to me in the waves when we drove down to the beach, all those billows rushing in. He exclaimed it in the foam swirling around my feet.

He didn't mention it or touch lightly on the subject. I'm telling you—He *yelled* it out. Spoke unmistakably through the sky, in case I didn't hear.

And now it resounds through my being. It's hard to believe it's true. That God would love me. Actually know me, *really know* me, and still would love me.

But He does, so He hollers it loud. To all of His children, He daily clamors it out. His *I love you* shout.

> *See what kind of love the Father has given to us, that we*
> *should be called children of God; and so we are.*
> 1 JOHN 3:1

> *For God so loved the world, that he gave his only Son, that*
> *whoever believes in him should not perish but have eternal*
> *life.*
> JOHN 3:16

HOW BEING A MOMMA HAS CHANGED ME

I DIDN'T KNOW HOW BEING A MOMMA would change me. When I quit working at the office and wondered if I'd miss all the grown-ups, I didn't know how much I'd be okay. It turned out I'd be fine teaching a little boy his letters and how to make friends and teaching a little girl how to paint with watercolors

and build a sand castle and gently scrub the grime from her baby doll's cheeks.

My email box got a lot thinner as the walls of my belly grew out and people weren't writing to ask me to do all these "important" things. But somehow I ended up finding all this delight in scrubbing mac and cheese off plastic Thomas the Tank Engine plates and changing little people's britches for the umpteenth time.

I really, really like being a momma.

I like the part where I get to cuddle up next to the little boy who grew big inside of me and gave me my first stretch marks, who continues to stretch my thinking with his questions like, "Does God ever get hungry?" and "What about sleep? Does God sleep?"

And I love the part where I push my little girl on the swing, even though I'd rather be reading a book or weeding the garden. And while she's learning to kick her legs out, I catch a glimpse of all that radiant light in her eyes and the way her silky, sun-streaked hair whooshes back and forth. I remember again what it was like to be young and wild and happy and free.

And I treasure the part where my baby smiles this great big, lively grin, his eyes glad and full of light, the moment he sees me peeking over his crib to scoop him up.

I didn't know how much I'd be giving my life away. Or that my most satisfying work would be when no one else was looking as I poured out all I had to nurture the lives of my babes. Or that God would be my strength as I learned to craft love, the stuff that lasts forever, a thousand times a day in a hundred different ways.

I didn't know how being a momma would cause me to care more for all the other boys and girls. That I'd begin to see them through a momma's eyes—this concern for their lives and a burden to help and protect them, too. I didn't know how my heart would hurt for the world when everyone else was fast asleep—how much I'd pray for God to push back the darkness. Or how much I'd ask Him to let His kingdom come here to this fallen world, like it is in heaven.

I certainly never knew how much I'd cry. All these happy tears. And how God would use a child's faith and purity to encourage me. How He'd show me anew, through such little people's eyes, how to view the world with all this wonder. Observing a caterpillar on a leaf. Stirring mud with a stick. Throwing rocks in a pond. Running for the sheer fun of it.

Sometimes when I look in the mirror and see how this tummy has warped and how these hips won't ever fit back into my favorite jeans I remember this—I get to be a momma.

> And the King will answer them, "Truly, I say to you, as you did it to one of the least of these my brothers, you did it to me."
>
> MATTHEW 25:40

WHEN IT'S HARD
TO REST

SOMETIMES WHEN I LAY SAMUEL DOWN FOR the night he fights. I'm not sure why he fights, because he's tired. But he keeps lifting his head up and he wails and he kicks and I have to put my hand on his head, ever so gently, and lay his head back down.

But still he fights. So we repeat this three or four times until he's completely exhausted and somehow, with the comfort of his momma close, he finally gives up and gives in and he finds sleep.

Then I make my way to my bed, stepping over the library books and the dirty clothes on the floor. I pull up the covers and turn out the lights and drift off to sleep. But then the middle of the night comes, and the cat meows, or Hope talks in her sleep, or Samuel wakes up again. So I get up and attend to something or someone and then I'm back in bed. Wide awake.

There's no good reason to be wide awake, because I'm tired. But I've got these worries and these fears, so I toss and turn and tell God about them and ask Him to help. And though I know He's big, somehow I've still got to hold on to things. Thankfully He does hear our tired, mumbling prayers, so before long, I sense His Presence near. I can almost feel the way He puts His hand on my head and gently lays it back down. Like He's saying, *I've got this. You can let go. You can let go and get some sleep.*

But I fight. And I contest. Because I don't want Him to forget about this certain thing and I forgot to mention that other thing. And so there we go, back and forth, me reminding God about the things I need Him to do and Him gently covering my head and saying, *I know. And I've got this.*

He's so tender this way. And somewhere in those wee hours, I relinquish control and abandon myself to the One who never sleeps. I think He wants me to know this universe is perfectly safe for me to live in. Because God doesn't ever leave me and

His love doesn't run out. There's no place where He doesn't show up or can't be found, so I can rest. Come what may, He'll use everything and He won't waste anything.

God takes the mire and muck of my suffering and uses it to sculpt me into the image of His Son. This is how my Maker, like a potter at the wheel, fashions the ugly into beautiful. This is what He says He will do for His children. For those who love Him—He'll work *all things* together for good (Rom. 8:28).

I want to believe Him. To gut-believe Him.

So I scribble it down and I speak it out loud. I sing it over my children and pray it into my own heart.

No matter what, I'll be okay. I can rest. He's got this.

> *I will both lie down in peace, and sleep;*
> *For You alone, O Lord, make me dwell in safety.*
> PSALM 4:8 NKJV

> *And we know that all things work together for good to*
> *those who love God, to those who are the called according*
> *to His purpose.*
> ROMANS 8:28 NKJV

LIGHT AND WHY IT
MOVES ME

LIGHT. I LOVE THE STUFF. LIKE, I'M crazy about it. Whenever it seeps its cheery self through my windows and pours itself out onto my floor or my chair or my anything—I'm mesmerized. This may sound strange, but I *crave* light. I get hungry for it. I think I know why.

Because light has a healing effect on me. It's like medicine for my insides. You see, I get bombarded from time to time with disparaging thoughts and pestering fears. I would rather be thought of as this always-cheerful, ever-optimistic, never-doubting-God kind of person. But the truth? I have some ugly moments. Times when I need to stop listening to myself and start talking to myself. I need to spend more time telling

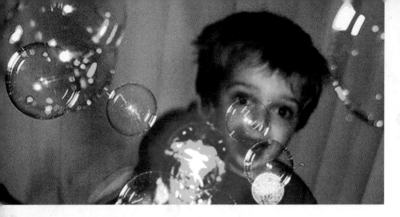

myself the truth. The truth that God is good. Always. And He never stops loving me. Ever. This truth that holds us fast in the blackest dark.

I learned light is made up of waves of energy. Perhaps that's why it moves me. All these cascading swells pulsing toward me, a pool of wonder.

I open wide the curtains every day to invite the gush of it in. Where it spills out on the carpet, that's where we sit and play. Where it moves, we move. We follow it. We bask in it. We drink it in.

It warms us. It encourages us. I'm telling you, it heals us.

You know what else I think is amazing about light? It transforms. It falls on ordinary things and turns them into art. When humdrum things are drenched in light, they become something worth beholding.

Gideon had informed me from the backseat, "Momma, do you know why God made the lightning? To show us how bright He is!" And it's true—God Himself says He's the Father of all the light. I love that about Him. Did you hear me? He is the source of *light*! And I love light. When I'm thinking about Him, gazing on Him with the eyes of my heart, I do feel it—the way He swallows up all my darkness.

It's hard living in this broken world. There is real evil and suffering, and it overwhelms. Oppressive thoughts, bad dreams . . . sometimes our worst fears actually do come true. Skeptics and believers—we all have this in common—this knowing grief firsthand. And God doesn't always make things right . . . *in this earthly life.* It does seem so unfair and unjust that our struggles with evil aren't always resolved here.

I confess I can get so terribly depressed when I pay much attention to these things. So I must tell myself some true things.

Evil and dark do not have the final say. God has the final say. And He is light. Beautiful, joy-bursting light. At the end of here and now, He wins!

He is so beautiful, isn't He? And so worthy, that I should live all my life before His light-bearing face. I'm basking in Him today.

> *This, in essence, is the message we heard from Christ and are passing on to you: God is light, pure light; there's not a trace of darkness in him.*
>
> 1 JOHN 1:5 THE MESSAGE

WHEN YOU WONDER
WHERE GOD IS

WHEN I WAS A LITTLE GIRL, BEFORE I was adopted, bad things happened. Because bad guys can live in foster homes and in neighborhoods, and sometimes they do wrong things to little people when no one else is looking.

When I was older—a teenager—and after I'd been rescued and had come to know Jesus, I still remembered those bad guys who had done the wrong things. And I wondered where God had been when I was so afraid.

I had learned God is good and He's kind, but I couldn't help but wonder why He let those things happen. Didn't He know I was too little to protect myself? Wasn't He merciful and strong? So one night I fought it out with my Maker. I asked Him hard questions and begged of Him answers.

Then I laid my head down on my pillow and cried. That's when Jesus came. The Comforter had heard my painful plea, and He came to bring me peace. The Good Shepherd drew gently near to this little broken lamb and opened my eyes to see that all the bad stuff that made me sad made Him sad, too. All the things that broke my heart broke His. He was there. He saw and He hurt, because what happens to the "least of these" happens to Him (Matt. 25:45).

God isn't aloof to our pain, nor does He stand far away. He's able to comfort because He once entered into our suffering and dark to take on all our aches. Jesus walked no easy road. When He went to the cross, God piled all the bad, unspeakable things of the whole, messed-up world on His perfect, spotless Son. Sin ripped His veins, tore His skin, and bloodied His back. Jesus was bruised so we could be made whole. It's by His wounds we get healed.

That night God whispered into my heart He would take the bad intended to harm me and use it for my good (Gen. 50:20). And He could take all the ugly meant to mar me and turn it into something beautiful. And as I lay there, heart wide open

to Him, He did take all the oppression designed to shackle me, and He set me free. Then He bound up my wounds.

I still have the memories, but He's taken away the shame. And there is a God who works all things together for good, for those who love Him. And if He works in all things, then doesn't that mean He doesn't waste anything? No evil? No dark? No pain? Since I've been dealt a little suffering, I do have this tender awareness of the hurting in others. I am aware in a way I couldn't be had I not experienced it in my own life.

When you wonder where God is, He's right here. Healing up the brokenhearted, holding on to the weeping, and quieting us with His love. And once we've been made whole and comforted deep, we can get up on our way and go do the same.

> *But he was pierced for our transgressions,*
> *he was crushed for our iniquities;*
> *the punishment that bought us peace was on him,*
> *and by his wounds we are healed.*
> ISAIAH 53:5 NIV

THIS LIFE—
A LOVE SONG

There have been nights (You know . . . You've seen, heard me)
when with the deepest ache I've reached out for You. Those
nights, with tears like little rivulets down my cheeks, when
I've longed, hurt, to feel You. To be held. I've thought if only I
could reach out far enough to touch You, holy You, or even the
hem of Your garment, I would be healed. Not just to *know* You
are there and You are real but to take hold of You. To feel Your
love, all-encompassing. I've wondered why there exists this
ache in my chest for more of You if You didn't intend to fill it.

And I have found, Lover of me, You *are* there and You are not
silent. And Your love pulses, moves toward me in a thousand

ways at every turn. I have but to stop, to cease striving, and listen. It's there in the stillness, when my heart is attentive and quiet, I'm able to hear the rhythmic beating of Yours.

Lord, You are a suffering Savior, knowing grief firsthand. Broken for me, You let my sins rip Your skin, tear Your veins, and crush Your brow. You were bruised up so I could be healed up. I know how lost I've been, wandered and strayed till my soul has wrought sore. Oh, but I've been sought after. You've come running, shouting, heading in my direction, and I've been found! What can I give You? What can I bring? A love song? I could sing to You with my life, my rescuing King!

Yes, I praise You. And I write it down so it can be known that on this day, when I was trying to get ahold of You, You were close. Close enough to feel. Could it be You were reaching out, too? That You were reaching out *first*? That You've even been there all along? That it's always been in Your heart I would find You? Feel You? Know You?

Though my lips are stammering, Lord, I belt it out. And is that You I hear singing, too? Calming me with Your love and rejoicing over me with Your songs? I tune my heart to the beat of Yours and give You all I've got to give—this life—my love song.

The Lord your God is in your midst,
a mighty one who will save;
he will rejoice over you with gladness;
he will quiet you with his love;
he will exult over you with loud singing.

ZEPHANIAH 3:17

You have said, "Seek My face."
My heart says to you,
"Your face, Lord, do I seek."

PSALM 27:8

WHEN YOU DON'T MEASURE UP

I FELT IT TWICE THIS WEEK. The *You're not good enough and you don't measure up* feeling. Once when I was with a couple of my good friends. We were standing there in the kitchen and I noticed how fit they were. How hip they dressed. And how beautiful they looked. And then I heard the little voice, *Um . . . you're a dweeb. You don't look like them. You don't fit in. You don't measure up.*

I only entertained the notion for a minute, because I recognized it for the sabotaging lie it was. I'm learning to pray about all the little things, so I told Jesus my thoughts and felt Him reassuring me . . . *Don't compare yourself with others, Maggie. It's not wise.* So I sat down and enjoyed my friends for who they

were and wondered how I could get my hair in little braids like one of them.

Then today I felt it again. A friend said something perfectly harmless about something I made and I read into it and kept reading into it until I was mad at the world all full of people who might not accept me or think I don't have what it takes. I was shaken. Because what do you do when you set out to create something beautiful and people don't like it? Do you crawl into a hole and attempt to drown the world out? Do you stomp the ground and tell everyone to shut up? Do you decide you'll never take another risk again? Seriously, I consider these things.

But Jesus whispered it sweetly again, *Maggie, don't compare. Don't compare yourself with others. It's not wise.* I think I know why. Because on the one hand I might compare myself and think I'm somehow better, and I might come out with a puffed-up head. On the other hand, I might compare myself and come out feeling like a doofus. Like I don't measure up or I'm not good enough, and it might sink me into despair. And Jesus doesn't want me to despair.

So instead of standing in front of the mirror repeating, *You are a rock star! There's no one like you!* I take God at His Word and decide it's not wise to compare. The world may get out the measuring sticks, judge, and condemn, but Christ is always there before God's throne standing up for me. Nothing, absolutely nothing, can separate me from the love of Him who intercedes and embraces all of me (Rom 8:38–39 paraphrase).

For we dare not class ourselves or compare ourselves with those who commend themselves. But they, measuring themselves by themselves, and comparing themselves among themselves, are not wise.

2 CORINTHIANS 10:12 NKJV

THE WAYS WE LOVE

SHE LOOKS UP AT ME WITH THOSE wildly happy eyes. She's painting because it's in her to create. She holds up her artwork to show me, to hear me say, "Whoa! That's a good job, Hope. Nice! You're a good artist." There's a way to speak into each other with words that help and heal. The kind that helps others grow stronger.

I could love her with my words.

Gideon makes the biggest mess. I could get on him for all the messes he makes. They seem unending. Or I could let some of those things go, knowing these mothering days will soon be folded up and tucked away. There are tones that nurture and accept. Tones that make a person feel safe.

I could love him with my voice.

Samuel looks at us intently at times, as though he's peering right through us. I fix my eyes on him too because there's no awkwardness between us—just this knowing and deep contentment. There's a way we hold each other with our gaze. Sometimes a look can embrace.

I could love him with my eyes.

> *Let the words of my mouth and the meditation of my heart*
> *be acceptable in your sight,*
> *O Lord, my rock and my redeemer.*
> PSALM 19:14

LOOKING FOR HELP

THIS MORNING I SAT ON THE COUCH a bit discouraged and asked God for help. I mustered up what faith I could (which didn't feel like much, at the moment) and whimpered it out.

Then I got up and trusted He would somehow come, this Maker of mine, and strengthen my heart and give me what I need to thrive in this new day.

And at the kitchen sink, as I scrubbed yesterday's grime, I heard it. No kidding—I heard it loud and clear. Sometimes the voice of Jesus can come in the form of your little boy whizzing by on his tricycle, shouting boisterously to his playmates, "Hey! If you get stuck, I'll help ya! And if you get hurt, *I'll help ya!* Okay?"

Thank You, Lord, for the countless ways You come. Often waiting till we're good and desperate. But You do come. As sure as the sun rises, You come to help the ones who feel their need.

I'm letting this promise ring through my heart today:

> *I lift up my eyes to the hills.*
> *From where does my help come?*
> *My help comes from the Lord,*
> *who made heaven and earth.*
>
> PSALM 121:1–2

WHY GOD DOES WANT
YOUR MESSY HEART

JESUS SAYS, COME (MATT. 11:28). I GET that. All day long I
tell my kids to come to me. They come with their snotty noses,
and I wipe them. Or they come with their grimy hands, and
I wash them. Or with their hungry bellies, and I give them
something good to eat, some sustenance to fill them up. So
when Jesus says *Come*, I know what He means. He means simply this: *Come with your messy self. I see you're hungry-hearted.
I know you're a wreck. Now come over here. Come, right now.
I've got what you need.*

I'm thankful Jesus is like that. And I'm glad He doesn't say,
*Wait. Wait till you've got it all together. Don't come near Me
with your messy heart. Fix yourself. Get it right. Dust yourself off*

and make yourself look good. And when you feel better because you look better, then you can come.

Jesus doesn't call the righteous do-gooders to come to Him. He doesn't beckon the impressive hoity-toities. He calls the broken and disheveled. The battered and scuffed up. You know, the ones who actually *need* Him. That would be me.

I'm also glad Jesus doesn't say, *Oh, and one more thing. You can come, but first you need to know some more stuff about Me. So take some time and fill your head plumb full of God-knowledge. Then when you know all the right things and you can spout out all the right answers, come.*

Because that's what the Pharisees did. They thought God would accept them if they knew lots of stuff and if they performed in all the right ways. But all their God-knowledge did

was puff them up and trip them up. They were too full of pride to come to Him with their messy hearts. In fact, they didn't even realize they *had* messy hearts.

So Jesus says come. And He calls the people who are tired, who've worn themselves out. The ones who have a lot on their minds and more than they realize on their hearts. The ones weighed down by life, exhausted from just living. And the neat thing is, the only criteria Jesus requires of us to come is to simply feel our need for Him. Because we're depleted. And we're a wreck. And we don't have what it takes.

This is the sweet promise He makes: *I'll give you rest.* And He does. He gives us soul rest.

So I come. I come to Him as I actually am so I can know Him as He actually is. The God who fills a hungry heart and satisfies it with Himself. The One who can take an anxious soul and calm and quiet us with His love. I don't wait till I'm better. I come. Because that's the way Jesus would have it.

This God who is always for us, always, *always* for us—He aims to give us rest.

> Come to Me, all you who labor and are heavy laden, and I will give you rest.
>
> MATTHEW 11:28 NKJV

HUNGER FOR BEAUTY

BRENT AND I HEAD OUT TO RUN some errands and, as we drive, I can't stop looking, gazing, scanning all the fields and all the ditches. I want to see every tree and every blazing bush and all the wildflowers: to take it all in, all the beauty.

The sky is the perfect saturated hue of blue-gray. It makes the splashes of yellow and orange and crimson stand out, so I can't stop saying, "Ohhh, look at that! Look at THAT!" I'm sure I'm becoming annoying, but I want him to see what I'm seeing.

I actually feel a pang that all too soon these brilliant leaves will be gone, and I don't want to miss even one moment of them! If I were crazy, I'd stop this car right here on the side of the road and jump out. Then I'd walk around slowly and give each tree my full attention, and I'd gather all those wild purple asters up and clutch them into a big bouquet for my kitchen table.

I wonder sometimes why it is I'm so ravishingly hungry for all this beauty. These eyes are never satisfied with one day's worth. I wake again and again yearning for more. What is it in me that compels my pursuit, no matter where I am?

Each morning I pull the window shades, anxious to see the splendor of a new day. Evening arrives and I can't settle into bed until I've slipped out the front door for one last peek at the milky-white moon.

Sometimes I walk out into the grocery store parking lot and, when I see the sky, I want to point up and shout out right there for everyone to hear, "Hey guys! Looky there! Do you see it? LOOK! The GLORY!"

Could it be I was always meant to be a beauty-hunter? A glory-gazer? That perhaps the God who made me and all this I see somehow tucked into me this longing? So maybe, just maybe I'd go looking . . . and searching . . . and pursuing . . . until I found the source that would satisfy all this beauty-hunger . . . *Him*.

And aren't all the beauty-hunters really God-seekers? The glory-starved on a pursuit to gather up more of Him?

So today here I am again on a quest to find beauty. This search drives me to the Source of where it all comes from. And I find all the while I've been out looking for beauty, I've been feeling my way toward Him.

The God who made the world and everything in it, being Lord of heaven and earth, does not live in temples made by man, nor is he served by human hands, as though he needed anything, since he himself gives to all mankind life and breath and everything. And he made from one man every nation of mankind to live on all the face of the earth, having determined allotted periods and the boundaries of their dwelling place, that they should seek God, and perhaps feel their way toward him and find him. Yet he is actually not far from each one of us, for "In him we live and move and have our being."

ACTS 17:24–28

WHAT EVERY GIRL
NEEDS TO HEAR

I WISH I COULD TELL YOU WHAT she means to me. How she doesn't have to do a thing to earn my love. I simply love her because she simply *is*. I've heard people say, "Oh, just wait till she's a teenager." Don't they know I plan to love her all the same? There's nothing so great she could do to make me love her more and nothing so terrible I would love her any less. After all, that's how my momma loves me. And isn't that how Jesus loves us?

I look at her, this little girl who miraculously came from me, and wonder what I was like when I was her age. Adopted when I was seven, I don't have any baby pictures and don't know where I was or who I was with when I was this little. Sometimes it does occur to me what a crazy wonder it is I'm right here . . . looking at her.

A girl needs so much. She needs to know she's loved. She needs to feel cherished, the whole of her embraced. She's got to feel secure and protected. She's got to be told she's a little beauty and she's precious. My heart aches for all the little girls who don't know. Who grow up their whole long life never believing that deep down.

So there are some things I'm going to have to whisper to her often. Some truths I'm going to pray will settle in deep. Because for some reason, girls have this way of forgetting. This tendency to not believe. We need some reassurance. There's a lot of other voices out there and they can be deafening. Discouraging. Depleting. Degrading. And before we know it, we're reaching out for something, *anything* to make us feel loved. To help us feel whole again.

So I'm going to tell her about her Maker—the One who thought her up to begin with. The One who fashioned and formed her. The One to whom she belongs. She's daily His delight. His mercies toward her are new every single dawning of every new day. She doesn't have to earn His love. He loves her simply because she *is*. And if she'll listen closely, she'll be able to hear Him—the way He sings over her His love song (Zeph. 3:17). Sometimes it's in the breeze and the sunlight on the grass. And sometimes it's in her momma's voice, her daddy's eyes, her brothers' laughter.

She'll need to know this Maker of hers keeps all her tears in a bottle (Ps. 56:8) and He's numbered the hairs on her head (Matt. 10:30) and He thinks of her more times in a day than all the sand on all the seashores in all the world (Ps. 139:17–18). I'll tell her, again and again, because I need to hear it, too.

And I'll pray this: in all her reaching out, her feeling along to take hold of something to satisfy the emptiness in her heart, she'll find *Him*. The One who completes her, makes her whole. Who gives a girl her value, her worth, beauty, joy, love. And may God give her the eyes to see He's been there the whole time, reaching out to pull her in.

> *You have kept count of my tossings;*
> *put my tears in your bottle.*
> *Are they not in your book?*
> PSALM 56:8

> *How precious to me are your thoughts, O God!*
> *How vast is the sum of them!*
> *If I would count them, they are more than the sand.*
> *I awake, and I am still with you.*
> PSALM 139:17–18

EXTRAVAGANT LOVE

SOMETIMES I CAN FEEL IT—THIS INCREDIBLE God-love
trickles down, water drops on a thirsty soul, saturating all of
me.

I reach out—it is wide. As far as the east is from the west.

I reach up and it is long. I test it. It holds.

Some days I can hear it, like a shout, clear out of the blue sky.
In a grocery store parking lot I look up and overhear Him
declaring it. His glory whooped and hollered all across the
heavens, making me aware He is. Was. Always will be.

Other times it's soft, like a whisper I can only hear when I'm
still. Quiet. Listening. But oh, how I hear it. The throbbing,

pulsing swoosh of His beating heart. It's absurd He would lavish love in all these ridiculous ways. A patch of chicory. Sometimes I hear it best in a patch of chicory. Little blue love letters. Dozens by the fence.

He speaks it to me day and night. A message always strumming, straight from His heart.

It falls new every morning and I am drenched. Wet through. And all I was looking for, I find. What I've been needing—it's right here! I open my hands—He gives me His heart.

Extravagant Love.

> *But God shows his love for us in that while we were still sinners, Christ died for us.*
> ROMANS 5:8

> *This is how God showed his love among us: He sent his one and only Son into the world that we might live through him. This is love: not that we loved God, but that he loved us and sent his Son as an atoning sacrifice for our sins.*
> 1 JOHN 4:9–10 NIV

WHEN YOU'VE
FORGOTTEN
YOU'RE ON THE
SAME TEAM

I LOVE MY HUSBAND VERY MUCH. HE'S truly the best friend
I have and, honestly, he's pretty easy to love. He works hard.
He comes home every night to be with us. He takes out the
trash. He mows the grass. He says "thank you" for dinner.
My goodness, he even keeps the lid down on the toilet. He's a
pretty swell guy. But sometimes I actually forget he's so great. I
start noticing all the things he's not doing that I was thinking
he should be doing. And then I get perturbed with him. And
by perturbed, I mean I stop liking him so much.

Resentment clouds my view and, since he doesn't measure up, I start thinking about how I can make him pay.

I know, I'll ignore him for the rest of the day. Or I'll stop doing his laundry and picking up his socks and see what he thinks about that. No wait . . . I won't make him any more meals. Yeah . . . that'll teach him.

Or sometimes the very worst thoughts come to my mind—*I'll leave him. I'll go away and make him feel the pain of loss.* Ouch.

When thoughts and feelings like these come, it *seems* like a good idea at the time to dwell on them until they become the way I live. It *seems* like the best thing to do is let my heart fill up with resentment and meanness. If I made him pay and got my way, then all would be better, right? Well, not really. A revengeful, unforgiving heart actually feels pretty terrible inside. And who wins if even one person chooses to stop loving the other?

So what am I to do when I mostly want to be mean? When I'd rather teach Brent a thing or two about not measuring up to all my expectations . . . even if they are a bit unrealistic?

All I know to do is pray. Because God, the One who formed our hearts, is the only One who can make an ugly heart good.

And can I tell you something? God is amazing! He hears our prayers! When I get stuck and desperately need Him to change my heart, He does! When I ask Him to help me forgive, He reminds me of how much He's forgiven me and then gives me the ability to forgive those little things that seem so big. When I ask Him to help me love again, He pours His love right into my heart so I have something to give to Brent.

Just when I was thinking the worst—God reminds me of something. I *need* Him for this marriage to work out. I *need* Him for this marriage to be strong. I *need* Him to keep me in it, because Brent and I—well, we're actually on the same team.

And it's a pretty wonderful thing to have a teammate. Especially a handsome one.

> *And hope does not put us to shame, because God's love has been poured into our hearts through the Holy Spirit who has been given to us.*
> ROMANS 5:5

WHEN IT'S HARD TO TRUST

GIDEON WRAPS HIS LITTLE HAND ROUND MY neck as I lay beside him and pleads, "Momma, will you stay with me?" It's thundering outside and it comforts him to fall asleep in the presence of another.

I tell him I'll stay for a minute but he'll be okay because he's got Jesus, who is always with him even when momma leaves. He mumbles, tired, "Jesus is sad because He wants us with Him."

I think about the God who feels pain because sometimes His children don't trust Him. We get scared, and in our fears we run away because tornadoes come. I know a man who was picked up by one, thrown across the yard, and killed. I had wondered how God could be so unkind.

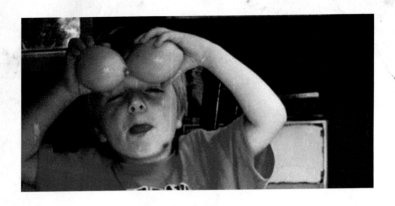

I drift off to sleep and awaken again to a rowdy rush of wind. I remember God in the dark, but instead of being comforted I'm afraid, because what if these walls give and all comes crashing, caving in on us? What do you make of a God who allows things you think you wouldn't allow, and where do you go when God doesn't feel safe?

We are hounded here by a devil who relentlessly lies, always accusing our Maker. He drills into us God is mean and a tyrant and He's holding out and He's not about to give us His best.

In the morning I get up while the house is still quiet and the rain has calmed itself into a drizzle. I sit on the couch and ask God questions. I read His words and look for His heart. I find it there on the page.

The Lord is good to all, and his mercy is over all that he has made.

PSALM 145:9

My emotions scream a hundred reasons why this can't be true. Because there are babies who break at the wrath of their parents and children who are sold as sex slaves. Bad guys hunt down to hurt others and cancer ravishes bodies and whirlwinds throw people around and there are those who die because hunger eats them away!

That ancient serpent taunts, "God isn't good," when the truth is this whole world is a reeling wreck because of sin. And isn't this why Jesus came?

There is a God who knows our pain. Jesus is the Savior who suffered, entering into our world filled with sin and evil and disarray. Christ took on the struggle and strain of our human condition so He could overcome sin and death and the Evil One. When Satan shrieks God isn't good and can't be trusted, we have only to look at the splintery cross where blood drained down and Love came running for all of us. God gave us His best when He sent His Son. God wants us with Him. No need for His children to run away. The rain spills down through gutters. His grace is seeping in.

> *Trust in him at all times, O people;*
> *pour out your heart before him;*
> *God is a refuge for us.*
> PSALM 62:8

WHAT A FAMILY
IS FOR

ALL OF US, WHEN WE FIRST ENTERED this world, were born into a family. At least that's the way it was *meant* to be. So the moment our first breath filled up our lungs, we belonged. To a family. As in, as soon as we're here, we're *in*. We're with them and they're with us. That's what family is for.

We all need this. We've got this hollow ache to belong, so God gave us some people to belong to. Now we don't usually get to pick those people. There's a saying, "You can pick your friends, but you can't pick your family." It's true. No family is perfect. We're all a bit dysfunctional. And some families are plain crazy. But we've been given each other, so we're all on a team and we keep picking each other. It's the one place where we can always fit in—not because of what we do, or how we look, or what we've got, but because of *whose* we are. We're each other's keeper.

A family is meant to nurture—to hold each other tight and to help each other grow. To make each other laugh and to speak words that build each other up. But like I said, no family is perfect. Sometimes we say the wrong things and we say some mean things. Sometimes we make each other cry. That's where forgiveness comes in. A family forgives, and we have to do it over and over again. Because we're meant to stick together, and the only way to stick together is to bear with one another long. Sometimes we're all we've got. So when we rub each other wrong, we try to make it right. We don't hold each other at arm's length or shove someone out. It's not easy, but we have to hang in there if we want to stay close.

And when someone in the family is weak, the stronger ones help them up. The stronger ones build them up. And they never, ever give up, because everybody at times is a bit weak and we all need a helping hand. That's why God gave us family.

Your family may be the only ones waiting up at night when you're out too late. Or praying late at night when you're far away. Family doesn't forget you're there, even when they can't see you. And they run after you, even if you try to push them away. If all the miles in between won't let them reach you, they'll chase you with their prayers. At least, that's the way a family is supposed to be.

And somehow our family, us all belonging, is a picture—a glimpse of a kingdom to come. A place where children of the King will come and never, ever be alone again. Until then, we keep reaching for each other and pulling close. We keep holding. We keep protecting. We keep forgiving and persevering. This is what knits us all together. We're anchored in the security of knowing we're *in*. As in, I've got you. You've got me. We're each other's. We belong. And that's what a family is all about.

> *Put on then, as God's chosen ones, holy and beloved, compassionate hearts, kindness, humility, meekness, and patience, bearing with one another and, if one has a complaint against another, forgiving each other; as the Lord has forgiven you, so you also must forgive.*
>
> COLOSSIANS 3:12–13

And when you run hard after Him, determined to find Him with that one speck of faith...

BECAUSE
SOMETIMES
LIFE HURTS

RIGHT NOW SAMUEL'S PAINS ARE SMALL AND seemingly insignificant.

He bumps his head. He gets a mosquito bite. He has to go to bed when everyone else is awake, and I think that hurts his feelings a little.

But all too soon he'll get older and experience deeper, more profound pain. I won't have to tell him the world is broken because he'll feel it. The weight will come and gradually bear down on his little shoulders.

I wish it weren't so. I wish I could always stand between him and the world and bear the brunt of it. I wish he would only have to know forever happiness. But before long he'll become acquainted with grief—the kind that presses in on the heart and dries out the bones. The world is not as it should be. This harsh reality will set in and put its ugly mark upon his soul.

Though I can't protect him in every way and shield him from pain, I can teach him some things to give him hope. He'll need to know there is Someone who tends to broken hearts and binds up wounds. There is a Person who entered into all the pain and misery, taking every bit upon Himself. There is a Healer. A Rescuer. Jesus.

There is this promise:

> *For I consider that the sufferings of this present time are not worth comparing with the glory that is to be revealed to us.*
> ROMANS 8:18

So I'll whisper to him in the dark, in those wakeful, anxious hours of the night, about the glory that's coming. How it doesn't make sense now, but one day he'll have new eyes to finally see the whole redeeming story—all the lost pieces coming together. Darkness will be light. There will be a day of reckoning when God will compensate in eternity the wrongs suffered here for a little while. One day these years, all these *aching* years, will be old tales.

And as he reaches out for answers, I'll sing him songs of hope—the songs of the redeemed. The King will wipe away all the tears from our eyes, and there'll be no more of anything that makes us afraid. Even death will die, and all that's sad and sickening will lay down, forever, in the grave.

> *I will seek the lost, and I will bring back the strayed, and I will bind up the injured, and I will strengthen the weak, and the fat and the strong I will destroy. I will feed them in justice.*
>
> EZEKIEL 34:16

> *And I heard a loud voice from the throne saying, "Behold, the dwelling place of God is with man. He will dwell with them, and they will be his people, and God himself will be with them as their God. He will wipe away every tear from their eyes, and death shall be no more, neither shall there be mourning, nor crying, nor pain anymore, for the former things have passed away."*
>
> REVELATION 21:3–4

HOW TO REALLY ENJOY YOUR LIFE

TAKE THIS DAY, THIS ONE NEW AND glorious day you've been given, and give thanks to the God who gives you all your days. Be ready for an adventure, because no matter how big or little you are, you can't know what the day will bring.

But you can choose to live all your moments fully present and fully aware all of life is *wonder*, and this will help you feel fully alive!

Take all the things in your heart that make you feel anxious or afraid or weighed down and give them to your Maker. Then breathe in . . . and breathe out . . . because your Heavenly Father is quite big enough and kind enough to care for you.

Kick your legs out and throw your head back, *waaaay* back, and enjoy the ride. And if you start to feel a little squeamish, yell out for help!

Your Maker is also big enough to hear you—all the way down here. And He'll be coming, with healing in His wings.

> *But to you who fear My name*
> *The Sun of Righteousness shall arise*
> *With healing in His wings.*
>
> MALACHI 4:2A NKJV

THE BEAUTY HUNT

I DON'T KNOW IF YOU'RE LIKE ME. If sometimes you're trudging along in life, making your to-do lists and checking them off. Scrubbing your floors and your commodes. Buying your groceries and cooking your meals. Sorting your mail and paying your bills. And basically going about your everyday, ordinary life. You crank out the tasks at hand so you can keep up with life, all the while trying hard not to measure your worth and value by the amount you're producing.

I don't know if you're like that or not. I don't know if you've ever wondered why we call ourselves human beings when we mostly feel like human doings.

And I don't know if you ever get this restless feeling inside, like there must be something more. Or if you have this itch in your chest to go out looking for beauty, to find it and gaze long at it and somehow be a part of it.

I do. There are these moments when I'm folding the laundry or doing the dishes or sitting at a desk and typing out the emails, that I can't take it any longer. I have to go on a beauty hunt. I've got to see the sky and feel the wind on my face and the dirt beneath my feet. Sometimes, I need to go on a walk with God and look at all the things He's made.

And when I do this—when I quit the worrying about producing and I put down the dish towel or shut off the computer and I head out to gaze at all the glory—I feel so alive! And though I never feel worthy to talk to God, He carved a way for me to always be able to come back to Him so I do. I talk to Him about whatever is right there on my heart and before I know it, I'm breathing deep and calm and wildly free.

And I can't help but wonder if my Maker tucked beauty-hunger down deep in my chest so I'd go tromping barefoot through a field to more vividly *see*.

I worship Him. Sometimes when I'm busy doing and sometimes when I'm enjoying *being*. After I've wandered with Him in a muddy field all filled up with sky it feels a little easier to go back to the to-do list. Because then I remember the One who calls Himself Emmanuel, whose name means *God with us*, really is here. His beauty is all around, adorning my gritty, grimy life.

> *For since the creation of the world God's invisible qualities—his eternal power and divine nature—have been clearly seen, being understood from what has been made, so that people are without excuse.*
>
> ROMANS 1:20 NIV

HOW WINTER HAS TAUGHT ME ABOUT THE KINGDOM

THE WINTER HAS BEEN MY TEACHER. THESE long, cold, drawn-out months. Snowstorm after snowstorm, the drifts piling up outside my door, filling up my view there at the kitchen window. A girl born and raised in the South can start to wonder if the warmth will ever come, if spring will actually return again.

Because there is this period right smack-dab in the dead of winter when there aren't any signs of any change coming, anything different on its way. Just this cold, bleak reality. There's no new life out there in the yard: just one little cardinal perched on the pine branch, wind blowing through his chest feathers. He clings, hopeful, in the middle of the frigid deadness and hardness all around him.

After a while, it's hard to wait. But still I wait, because in the recesses of my heart I've got this hope. Have you ever noticed on the coldest winter nights the stars seem to shine the brightest? I keep waiting because I know underneath all the cold, in the deep dark of the soil, there's life. It's all quiet and still and resting for now, but I've got this promise inevitably spring *will* come and life will break out with a triumphant unfurling—it's only a matter of time. And the longer I wait, the greater the anticipation.

These northern winters have taught me a lot about God's kingdom. The sons and daughters of the King, we walk by faith here and not by sight. The world seems awfully bleak, and the doubting, unbelieving, cynical wind cuts us through and threatens to seep right into our bones. There are these long, drawn-out seasons when there's no sign of a single thing changing, or anything different on the way. But we've got this seed of eternity planted down deep in the fertile soil of our hearts, so we can't help but long for the warmth and light of the kingdom full of the Son.

And every once in a while we look up to see the shadows shift and the light change. And if we're quiet and still enough and tuned in, we can sometimes hear it—the ebbing, pulsing rhythm, slow and steady like a distant drum. We feel it now and then, the swelling of forever-life waiting to burst out. This mystery of already and not yet. Of here now, but not fully realized.

Because one day, God's glory light *will* split the blackest dark and the kingdom chorus will ricochet through the cosmos and the children of the King will dance giddy-glad and barefoot on the warm shores of God's eternal reign.

For now we wait.

Outside, the cardinal chirrups and something in me stirs, as if I recognize an echo of a tune from a faraway place. A drift of snow falls from the pines and I smile quiet. There's this slow and steady melting, this thawing out of what's been frozen through and slumbering. A new season is coming. The hope of spring.

> *And giving joyful thanks to the Father, who has qualified you to share in the inheritance of his holy people in the kingdom of light. For he has rescued us from the dominion of darkness and brought us into the kingdom of the Son he loves.*
>
> COLOSSIANS 1:12–13 NIV

WHEN YOU'RE TIRED
AND NEED SOME REST

HE TELLS ME HE ISN'T TIRED. AND he's pretty persuasive—
except the part where he's wailing over little things, and he's
snappy, and he yells at his momma. I tell him not to yell at his
momma, but he yells again and then he sobs in his highchair
because he just bit his finger. I'd like to yell back, and sometimes I do, but this time I scoop him up and cradle him close.
Because when you've been loved, you learn how to love—you
find a way to embrace the one who kicks and screams.

I carry his sobbing self right up to his bed while he howls with
promises he's not tired, not one bit. But I don't listen to him
because I'm the momma, and I know a thing or two about
needing sleep. It's kind of funny, really, how the more adamant

he is that he's absolutely, definitely, for sure *not* going to take a nap . . . the quicker he goes and the longer he's out.

While he sleeps I think about rest. A different kind, though, that doesn't come from soft blankets and comfy pillows and a little shut-eye. It's the soul-rest that comes from the God who formed me, a God who knows me, a God who cradles me close: when I'm soul-weary and need to be held, when I've been stressing and striving and whining and fighting. But with a little faith, I lean into Him and find Him *there*. He lavishes crazy love undeserving on the ones who kick and scream.

I confess, I'm always surprised to find Him there, bringing me peace and comfort in the middle of all my mess. But His love is all around. So I rest.

> *And he said, "My presence will go with you, and I will give you rest."*
> EXODUS 33:14

> *Truly my soul finds rest in God;*
> *my salvation comes from him.*
> *Truly he is my rock and my salvation;*
> *he is my fortress, I will never be shaken.*
> PSALM 62:1–2 NIV

PERHAPS ALL GOD REALLY WANTS FROM US

I HAD A MOMENT ONE MORNING WHEN I was walking at breakneck speeds on the treadmill (not really), and I looked out the window at the snow gently blowing down and yelled to God, "We're doing it! I'm on the treadmill! WE'RE DOING IT!"

And then I started to weep, right there on the treadmill. I'm glad I didn't fall off. I cried because in one jubilant moment I realized the sweetest thing: I had been asking God to help me become motivated to exercise, and there we were and I felt like we were doing it together. I mean, I wouldn't have gotten on that thing if He hadn't answered my feeble little petition. I hate treadmills. I hate exercising. I like cookies.

And then it occurred to me God had been doing a lot of things with me. Like this whole *mothering* thing, and this whole *living life* thing. Do you know how many times a day I ask Him for help? For grace? For strength, wisdom, joy? And every once in a while I look up to see He's been helping me all along, walking right there beside me. He's faithful like that.

Now you might think it strange I'm claiming the God of the universe does things with me, but this is exactly what He aims to do. We don't have to wait till heaven to be with God. We can live with Him here.

Our Maker won't be segregated to Sundays, nor will He be poked down into a box until we've been good enough or have it together enough to allow Him in. He wants to be smack-dab in the middle of our everyday mundane, and He has every right to step across the property lines we draw on our time and scribble round the edges of our hearts.

After all, God made us and this whole place. He who framed the worlds and holds everything together by His power exists as the center of all things. And yet He's not indifferent to our

needs or afraid He'll somehow be defiled by our messy hearts. Jesus didn't lift the fringes of His garment and tiptoe around the mire and muck. He got His clothes dirty and His feet muddy, and He reached out and touched the unclean.

When Christ went back to heaven, He sent us His Spirit so whatever we do, we do it *with Him*. Is there anything too menial He won't help us with, or mundane that He won't be with us in?

I'm in the middle of washing dishes when my little Hope girl wants to "help." Here she comes with those eager eyes and the clunky chair and her elbows. And I get frustrated because I can't go nearly as quickly because she's awfully slow at handing me the bowls and the chair is actually taking up all the room. But I've asked my Maker to help me love her, so even at a sink full of sticky plates He enters in. I hear His voice, *It's okay, Maggie, to slow down. She's more important than the dishes. Go ahead and nurture her helpful spirit. I want her to help the world. It all starts right here at the kitchen sink.*

I wonder if this is all God wants from us—to live the whole of our lives with Him. This God who made the universe—He isn't very far away. Every now and then, after all the pleading for Him and all the asking, we sense He's been walking right beside us all along. And so we shout, *We're doing it! God, we're doing this together!* Perhaps it's the sweetest thing a human heart can feel. Us with Him.

> *And I will ask the Father, and he will give you another Helper, to be with you forever, even the Spirit of truth, whom the world cannot receive, because it neither sees him nor knows him. You know him, for he dwells with you and will be in you.*
>
> JOHN 14:16–17

BRAVE

ON CHRISTMAS DAY THE SKY BLED. I ran out the front door, outside in the cold to watch the crimson hemorrhaging out. I shivered, alive. The wind stung my nose and my ears and my fingers, but I had to see it because the sky doesn't bleed often and it never bleeds long before all the colors and light are gone. You could miss it if you don't stop for a spell.

I thought it interesting the sky was all ablaze on Christmas Day. This day when Jesus-followers pause and reflect on the way He came to live with us. Every year we read the story and sing the songs about how He came so humble, wrapped up in rags, inhaling the scents of a barn. And we remind ourselves about the whole point of His coming. How He journeyed to the cross, the red hot of His love bleeding out, to wash our

sin-soaked souls so we could be saved. I can't help but think of this as crimson plasma spills out across the sky.

Several days pass and I contemplate a new year and wonder with excitement what sort of adventure or adversity will come my way. And I think I want to name my new year. I'd like to name it "Brave." Brave because I'm not. Mostly, I'm not. Not when I turn on the news. Not when I think of my babes and the world they'll grow up in. Not when I look at our country and think of all the debt and the mess we've made.

All too often this little heart gets scared of what it can't yet see. And I wonder this: Can a God who isn't afraid, who is never afraid, who knows the end from the beginning, who made this sky and those trees, the God who made *me*—can He make me brave? Because this is what I want as I step into another year. I want to be brave.

I could acquire some crazy courage if I consider the brevity of it all—this one fleeting life. And I could walk down this new road unafraid if I recall God is the biggest! He's the strongest! He's always right here with me! How can my heart pound panic if I remember there is a forever and in the end He wins?

So I'll meditate on some truths:

Don't panic. I'm with you.
There's no need to fear for I'm your God.
I'll give you strength. I'll help you.
I'll hold you steady, keep a firm grip on you.
ISAIAH 41:10B THE MESSAGE

Cast all your anxiety on him because he cares for you.
1 PETER 5:7 NIV

God is our refuge and strength,
a very present help in trouble.
PSALM 46:1

And I'll step out with a brave-hearted belief in the heart of a good God, though I don't yet see and I may not understand. God works through everything, and He wastes nothing. This God who bled can make a scared girl brave.

A PRAYER TO THE GOD OF MY LIFE

I WALK HERE IN SHADOWED LANDS, THIS valley hemmed in by uncertainties. Lord, You've got to open up my eyes, those eyes of my heart that see through all this life, through this dusty pane, to another realm. I need eyes to see Your glory, the ways You shine Your kingdom light into the world.

So much of my life I've walked blind, oblivious to the ways You show up, and deaf to the undertones of Your voice. That melody always reverberating You exist and You are a Rewarder of those who look for You to find You. To find You here in all our rubble.

Lord, if You don't open my eyes, how else will I see? How will I see the thread of redemption that runs through all my days,

through all of time? That string of grace that stitches all the pieces together? That scarlet cord held out to even the chief of sinners?

And Lord, would You take the hardness off my heart? This unbelief and doubt. This hell-bent proneness to have it my way or no way. This ludicrous notion that if I clench my fists a little tighter I can actually be in control here.

I have got to *feel* You here. The warmth of Your breath on my face. The pulse of Your heart keeping the rhythm through all creation—Yours is a love everlasting. The faithful kind that pursues until the end, knowing full well there's no end in sight.

I've got to *know* You here. To learn Your language. To rely on Your heart when I don't get Your ways. There are wrongs suffered here and it perplexes me. I need to know deep down in my gut You are good. You are *always* good. And You are always good to *me*.

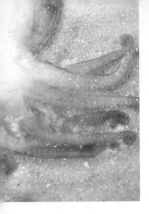

Lord, I see but dimly. Keep me from the skeptical belief that this shadowed valley I walk through is all there is. That this one fleeting life is worthless and trivial and then there is nothing.

Keep shining Your forever light into all my days, my ordinary moments. Let Your blaze break through my dark, making my path like the sun that shines ever brighter until the perfect day. That unending day when I'll wake up at last to the most real Reality. The Great *I AM*. All Your glory before my face.

> *I love those who love me,*
> *and those who seek me diligently find me.*
>
> PROVERBS 8:17

> *Now faith is the assurance of things hoped for, the conviction of things not seen.*
>
> HEBREWS 11:1

WHEN YOUR LIFE IS MOSTLY FULL OF ORDINARY THINGS

THE SUN GLEAMS AND WARMS MY FACE as March breezes blow. Daffodils nod.

Hope slides down her little, orange slide and plops to the ground. Eyes squinting, hair blowing, she braves the wind and goes at it again.

Gideon sits barefoot on cool sand in his turtle sandbox and digs, little lips rumbling the noise of toy trucks pushing heaps of dirt, mounding up, piling high, and flattening again.

Samuel lies on a pallet in the grass and reaches for his toes. Then turns and stretches out as far as his little hand can reach to grab hold of that one gossamer dandelion tuft.

Birds sing. Bees drone. The earth turns in this steady pace on its course around the sun. And all the while, God exists.

While I sit and read.

I wonder if we should build a fence around the backyard and where exactly to plant a garden and how to scare off those pesky woodpeckers beating holes into the siding of our house.

Hope gets stuck and cries, Gideon yells for me to watch his trucks work, and a plastic bucket blows onto the road.

God exists. And I sit a spell to breathe in spring.

I fold laundry, pick up scattered toys, wonder how to organize this place. I call Brent at work to ask him when he's coming home for lunch.

God exists.

I feed the goldfish.

And sometimes it hits me as strange. Not that God exists, but that God exists and my day is full of all these ordinary things. Since God exists—the God who spoke and there was light, who formed all us earth children from the dust of the ground, a God who always is and always was, who bent down to breathe life into our very lungs—shouldn't we be doing something else?

I rinse out a sippy cup.

But there is this:

> *So, whether you eat or drink, or whatever you do, do all to the glory of God.*
> 1 CORINTHIANS 10:31

And this:

> *Be still, and know that I am God.*
> PSALM 46:10

And when God made me, didn't He know most of my life would be eating and drinking and sleeping and cleaning? And since He exists, shouldn't that change the way I go about all my eating and drinking and everyday doing? My in and out, just living?

And since the angels in heaven always worship Him, those brilliant otherworldly creatures who never doubt He just *is*, shouldn't I be worshiping Him, too? When I'm at the sink and in the middle of the laundry, when I'm doing the holding and when I'm being held?

And shouldn't I be still and quiet in my heart with a reverent sort of awe of Him, even in the rush of things, simply because He exists?

God exists.

Is there any such thing as ordinary?

This awareness of Him in the humdrum of life—it changes everything.

> *And without faith it is impossible to please God, because anyone who comes to him must believe that he exists and that he rewards those who earnestly seek him.*
> HEBREWS 11:6 NIV

SOLID GROUND

TODAY STORM CLOUDS TUMBLE ACROSS THE SKY. Not just that big space I see outside my window when I look up. But in here, in my heart. Shadows shift across the lawn. My feelings flux. The world is made up of all these changeable things. People up and move away. Governments turn. Even the ground moves and shakes. Sometimes I get dizzy living with all these variables, and I feel a bit unsettled. There are those terrifying moments when I realize that as much as I try, I can't manage everything. I'm too small. Life feels too unstable. I cry.

I cry because my emotions are fragile and all mixed up. I cry because someone I love had the rug pulled out from under them and they're trying hard just to stand up. I cry because the world keeps spinning and sometimes it quakes and we're little people. It's scary when we're not in control here.

When shadows lengthen and skies gray up and thunder rumbles and my whole world rattles and shakes, I need some good news. Some truth to keep my soul from staggering. So I go looking for comfort, and I find it. Or shall I say, I find *Him*. There is a God who comforts and a truth that keeps me anchored. I'm not left alone here, and beneath these wobbly feet of mine I've got some sturdy terrain.

God is a firm foundation. An immovable, unshakable rock. So I cling to Him and I'm steadied. I build my life on Him, and I am secure because He's the one secure thing. I need a place for these feet to stand that won't erode when the rains come. That won't give way when the earth splits open wide. Everything else totters and fluctuates, but not Him. He is the same yesterday, today, forever.

So I come to Him another day and I build on Him. The whole of my life, I lay it all out there—give Him all I've got. This is my consolation in a world that teeters and sways—the ever-faithful One is with me here and He remains. So I rest on Him, a sure foundation. He is solid ground.

I love you, God—
you make me strong.
God is bedrock under my feet,
the castle in which I live,
my rescuing knight.
My God—the high crag
where I run for dear life,
hiding behind the boulders,
safe in the granite hideout.

PSALM 18:1-2 THE MESSAGE

Everyone then who hears these words of mine and does
them will be like a wise man who built his house on the
rock. And the rain fell, and the floods came, and the winds
blew and beat on that house, but it did not fall, because it
had been founded on the rock.

MATTHEW 7:24-25

WHEN YOU'RE AFRAID OF BEING ABANDONED

EVERY DAY IT SEEMS LIKE I STRUGGLE with a fear of some sort. Lately I've been taking them to God and asking Him about them, and every once in a while an answer comes flying. His Spirit is like a needle piercing through my muddled mess, and His love the thread that binds up my wound.

Just yesterday I told God about my biggest angst—someday I'm afraid He'll up and walk right out on me. I had told Him the honest truth: though I believe He's here with me now, deep down I imagine He'll abandon me right when my darkest moment comes. There's the "what if" that haunts me like a plague. *What if* when I need Him most, He turns His back and hightails it the other way? What if He leaves me without light and without hope and all alone?

Sometimes my faith hardly resembles a mustard seed.

But I had taken this fear to God and asked Him for help. And you know what? He came. In the strangest way, He came. And this is how—in vivid colors of childhood memories.

I must have been about three or four. Because I was just a little thing standing there in the grass, peering down the blacktop street. My birth momma had left me, and it wasn't the first time she'd left me, but this time at a relative's house. So I kept watching and I kept waiting, that little heart of mine yearning for her to come walking around the bend and back to me. I'd go find my aunt and, with a hollow pang in my chest, I'd ask if *this* was the day she was coming, but every time she'd shake her head. So I waited. My eyes glued to the bend in the road, because surely she was on her way. So I kept hoping.

Then another memory came: this time I was sitting in a social worker's office. Two of them were discussing how my mom had left, time and again had left, and as they talked in hushed tones about her issues I pretended not to hear. They'd look

at me out of the corner of their eyes as I kept playing on the carpet feeling lost and so alone.

Those pictures flooded my mind like they had several times before, but this time I saw things a little differently. Now I don't pretend to understand the mystery of all the hows and whys but I wondered, quietly I wondered: if my momma hadn't left me, would I be *here* today? And I know it's strange to say, but yesterday I caught this glimpse—that in all her leaving, Jesus came.

I acquainted myself with Him again. The God who says He'll never walk away. The One who promises to be with me always, even to the end of the age (Matt. 28:20). He is with me in the light, He'll be with me in the dark. He's my very present help in trouble. My faith grows bigger in the God who doesn't forsake.

> *For my father and my mother have forsaken me,*
> *but the Lord will take me in.*
>
> PSALM 27:10

THE MOST
IMPORTANT
THING

GOD CARES MOST ABOUT MY HEART. YOU know, the part of me on the inside that makes up who I actually am. Not my doing, but my *being*. My real self. God cares the most about that.

But sometimes I get confused and I think He cares the most about my *doing*. So I muster up some strength to do what I think I *ought* to do. And I try hard to make sure I do enough. And then I check my to-do list and I look in the mirror and see if I've measured up. And if I've done good, then I stand proud and puffed up. But if I've failed, I hang my head and get all depressed and in a funk. And all the while, I've missed the point: God isn't after my doing.

He's after my heart.

Because from my heart comes *everything*—all the issues of life (Proverbs 4:23). So that's what makes my heart important. Because life starts there, on my insides.

And since my heart is so important, then it's essential I do a heart check. I ask myself, What does Jesus require of my heart? He requires some things. Well, mostly He requires one thing . . . one outlandish thing. He requires my heart. All of it. That's all. No biggie. Just my whole, entire, real self. All my insides. Which is basically everything I've got.

And since He made me, He has claim on me. I belong to the One who laid down His life for mine, who purchased me with His blood. Not so that He could rule over me in some domineering dictator sort of way. But so that He could fill me with His life-giving Spirit, gently woo me by His all-encompassing love.

And since I've come to know Him, that He is indeed good and always for me, I do really want to give Him my heart. My whole, entire self. So I do. Though I have to do it again and again because there's something in me that wants to keep taking it back. I think part of it is fear. And part of it is this urge to be in control. And part of it is doubt and unbelief. Because if I always trusted

God and unceasingly believed Him, then of course I would run after Him with all of myself and never turn back again.

He is my heart's true home.

All throughout the day Jesus says, *Come to Me*. So I come and I don't hold back. I bring Him my heart, the part of me He's after, and I hand it right over. I do it again and again.

At the sink.

Over the laundry.

In the parking lot.

In front of the computer.

This is my most important thing—to escort my heart back home to the Maker of hearts and the Lover of me.

> *And he said to him, "You shall love the Lord your God with all your heart and with all your soul and with all your mind. This is the great and first commandment. And a second is like it: You shall love your neighbor as yourself. On these commandments depend all the Law and the Prophets."*

MATTHEW 22:37–40

WHEN YOUR LIFE IS REALLY WRECKY

EVERY DAY I DO ALL THIS CLEANING. And it doesn't even matter how spic-and-span I get the place the day before; a new day comes and it's not long at all before we've got a big ol' mess on our hands. That's the way life works. If I wanted to get all scientific and smart on you, I'd refer to this never-ending disarray as the law of entropy: second law of thermodynamics, I believe. Things always tend toward disorder. Always. You've got to expend some energy if you want to make them right again.

And quite honestly, I get kind of tired of it. It wears me out. But I've been learning something pretty neat. I'm learning every time I pick up a toy or scrub a toilet or dust an end table,

I'm actually preaching the gospel to myself. I'm telling a story of something to come. Something that's not all the way here yet but well on its way.

Because the long and short of it is, this whole wide, chaotic, broken world will someday be made right again. There's a kingdom coming and one day it'll all be fixed. There will come a time when everything will return to perfect and complete peace. Because that's what Jesus came to do and that's what He promises will happen. There, at the end of the here and now. That's a beautiful story. A story worth telling myself when I sort laundry.

So I wash the sink out and remember He'll wash this whole place clean. And I glue together a broken toy and remember He'll repair all that's been ruined. I put the puzzles together for the umpteenth time and remember one day all the pieces of this broken world will be put back together *in Him.*

That's what redemption is—God making everything right again. I long for that. With the deepest ache I long for it. I wait with eager hope and expectation, knowing full well God is re-making the world and building a kingdom. One day all things will become new and be made whole.

That makes cleaning not so hard. It actually even transforms it into a way to worship. To worship the God who entered into the wreck in order to restore *shalom. Perfect peace. Confounding completeness. Utter fullness. Absolute soundness. Total tranquility. Deepest rest.*

So I take a deep breath and pick up around here. And somehow, in restoring order from the wreck, I live out the sweetest story I know.

> *And he who was seated on the throne said, "Behold, I am making all things new." Also he said, "Write this down, for these words are trustworthy and true."*
>
> REVELATION 21:5

He will show up.
He who calls Himself the
Great I AM ricochets His love
out through the skies
and right into your
everyday mundane.

THOUGHTS ON THE KINGDOM

Gideon cried out for me in the middle of the night, when the moon was gleaming and the crickets were chirping, and I went quickly, stumbling down the hall to his room. Because when you love someone to the gleaming moon and back, you don't much care about your sleep, you want to comfort them.

He was crying and wanted to hide, and when I asked him why, he said he was scared of yelling lions. I've never been scared of yelling lions, but I've been afraid of lots of other things, so I brought him some chocolate milk in his sippy cup and we cuddled close. Then I told him softly that when he's scared, he can run to Jesus in his heart because Jesus is a hiding place. I know about that hiding place because even grown-ups get scared of things real and not so real, and we all need a refuge, so that's where I go running.

Gideon sipped his "chocky" and asked me if heaven was inside or outside. I had to smile, because kids have this way of reminding us how much we don't actually know. But I thought for a moment and told him I thought it was *both* because God says heaven is a kingdom and aren't kingdoms made up of houses and lands? Then I told him how God is a like a Lion King (Rev. 5:5), a good and strong one, and all the other mean, bad lions are afraid of Him. Gideon lay still enough to drift off to sleep, perhaps dreaming about the good Lion scaring all the noisy, yelling ones away. I found my way back to my pillow, and thought about the kingdom.

Because I had read Jesus' words, and He says His kingdom is coming and even now, it's come. But I look around and see a wrecked-up world. A place cursed by sin and fallen, all of us fallen, and things are not as they should be. We all carry around the weight of the curse. That's why there are little boys who wake up afraid of yelling lions, and why we're not always safe on the streets or in our own beds, and why there are those who suffer from unspeakably horrific things.

But there are these traces of what once was, of a place God first created and called good. We see beauty and experience love and are arrested by wonder. These whispers of the past echo through our days, and something deep inside us remembers how it used to be. We all hope for a better day. We long for paradise—a place where a noble, lionhearted King reigns and peace prevails. We want all the good to win and for Someone to come and make things right again. We feel around for some sort of Rescuer to take away our fears and redeem what's been lost so our souls can soar unfettered and free.

Jesus arrives on the scene of broken humanity, and He makes such audacious claims. He says He's coming again to make all things new. I believe Him who died to heal the world and all our wounds. He whose light ruptured through the dark and burst from the grave—He's *very much alive* and He isn't far away!

I confess I don't understand it all. There's so much I don't get and can't wrap my mind around. But with faith I cling to the King of all the kings and I run to Him. A Lion. A Refuge. A Hiding Place.

There are things unseen but real. God is here. His kingdom has come. I think on these things.

You are a hiding place for me;
you preserve me from trouble;
you surround me with shouts of deliverance.

PSALM 32:7

So we fix our eyes not on what is seen, but on what is
unseen, since what is seen is temporary, but what is unseen
is eternal.

2 CORINTHIANS 4:18 NIV

LEARNING TO LIVE
HERE UNAFRAID

SOME MORNINGS I WAKE UP ALL TROUBLED and fragile inside, as if the slightest nudge would upend me, send me toppling over into a brimful of tears. Sometime in the night fear reared his ugly head again, and I let him set up camp with me only to find he came, as always, strictly to torment—taking over like a tyrant.

When will I remember I'm not supposed to flee ahead? Fleeing ahead into all the "what ifs" always sends me reeling, panic-stricken, swallowed up by insecurity and despair. I must have some sort of soul-amnesia. I keep forgetting the truths that set me free, the truth that keeps me breathing in and out, un-afraid.

So I turn again to the Word, and I lay it over the topsy-turvy grid of my life. I look for the Center. I find Him there, and He reorients me. I read it slowly; somehow I've got to get it this time:

> But in these last days he has spoken to us by his Son, whom he appointed the heir of all things, **through whom also he created the world.** He is the radiance of the glory of God and the exact imprint of his nature, and he **upholds the universe by the word of his power.**
>
> HEBREWS 1:2–3

Did you hear that, little soul? There is a Maker who framed the worlds. A God who got everything started and keeps everything going. Why do I live as if He's some absentee landlord who left the world to spin in vain? He holds all things together by His *Word*. The Word crafted all this—stars, atoms, ocean, beetles, me. And the Word holds it all together. And who is this Word? I read it there on the page. The Word is God who became a Man—Jesus (John 1).

My lungs fill up with air. My heart fills up with praise. Those shadows are overcome by light and I'm seeing clearly now. There at the center is a God whose heart is for me, not against me. I have only to look at the blood red of the cross to verify that. A God who holds everything together is a good God, full of love. It's a slow journey, my friends, but I dare to say I'm learning how to trust Him. I'm learning how to live here unafraid.

> *The Lord is my light and my salvation;*
> *whom shall I fear?*
> *The Lord is the stronghold of my life;*
> *of whom shall I be afraid?*
>
> PSALM 27:1

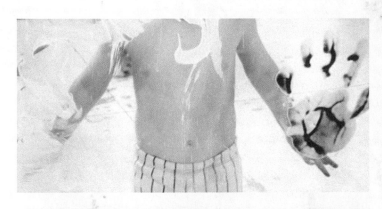

THE SOUND OF
OUR BREATHING

I CAN'T HELP BUT REMEMBER HIM—MY BIRTH dad. The last I
saw him I was four, maybe five. He was kind and gentle. Now
he was a wreck, yes, but I could tell he loved me and my little
brother best he could for the state he was in.

When he was sober and sound, he was tender and attentive. I
remember the time we danced, he and I. He had bowed and
I had curtsied, and he laughed because he'd never taught me
that—how to curtsey. Somehow, my little-girl heart just knew.
He showed me how to use the record player, so I would sit up
on the dresser and play records for hours.

But he left, and he kept leaving. He was running. Running from things he couldn't seem to keep away. Finally, I lost him completely. Years passed, and I grew up with kids of my own, but I never stopped wondering where he went or if he was okay. Then one night, a birth sister contacted me and she told me if I wanted to talk to our birth dad, I should call him soon because he was sick and about to pass away.

So I did. I called him up in the hospice house because I had never forgotten him. And sure, he'd done some wrong things and some stupid things, but in the last moments of his broken life I wanted him to feel the love of Jesus and lavish on him God's grace.

I called but he was too weak to do any talking, so I sat there and listened to him breathe. He tried to wheeze out words, but there was just this gasping and breaking. I knew what he meant. That he had loved us, the best he could for the state he was in. I sang him lines of "Amazing Grace."

I remember how I used to lay my head on his chest at night, falling asleep to the rise and fall of each new breath. And long after I was grown and he was gone, I had read that one of God's names is YHWH. Hebrew scholars tell us those four letters that make up His name are actually the sounds of *breathing*. I wonder at the generosity of a God who gives Himself a name we can't help but speak the moment we first enter the world and in those last few moments we lie resting, perhaps on a hospice bed.

My birth dad died a few days later, but I know he went in peace. And I marveled God would give me this—the One who made me would hear and remember all my little-girl prayers. God, who breathed out the stars and His very life into our chests, had let me see all along, when my birth parents were making a mess of things, that He was redeeming. He takes brokenness and remakes it into such beautiful things.

> *By the word of the Lord the heavens were made,*
> *their starry host by the breath of his mouth.*
> PSALM 33:6 NIV

> *The Spirit of God has made me,*
> *and the breath of the Almighty gives me life.*
> JOB 33:4

WHEN DADDIES AND THEIR BOYS GET MAD AT EACH OTHER

I WATCHED THE TWO OF THEM AS they hashed it out. The big guy wanting the little guy to obey. The little guy wanting to do something else, so he yelled and told his daddy to go back to work. It wasn't the first time he'd said it, so it hurt all the more. So the daddy sat dejected on the couch and the little guy tried explaining himself in his bed. "Mommy, sometimes daddies get mad at their boys and so their boys get mad at their daddies." I suppose these things have gone on as long as people have existed. These rifts in relationships. There are times when it hurts to love. It seems easier to hold each other at arm's length.

Around here, we're all a mess, so we ask God for help. Since He made us, we figure He knows how to operate life best. And when we're in a heap of trouble or we're just plumb stuck, we ask God to come. Sometimes it's a quiet begging in our hearts while we're sitting in pain on the couch. The good news is, the Helper always comes and shows us the way.

Later I watched them again, this time the little guy on the big guy's lap, both of them talking, trying hard to understand each other. Because instead of shoving the little guy away, the daddy pushed through his pain and put aside his pride to go after his little boy's heart. And the momma, she caught a glimpse of what Jesus is like—the way He bends down and draws close to listen. The way He pushes past all the muddled mess and moves toward the part of us that matters most.

And this morning, before he headed off to work, I heard the daddy speak it gentle to the little guy: "It's hard being a person. But we'll stick together, okay?"

Because love forgives and love forbears, and this is Jesus in us. We keep running *toward* even if it seems easier to push away.

And so long as we all have each other, I suppose we'll get to practice this the rest of our days.

Love is patient, love is kind. It does not envy, it does not boast, it is not proud. It does not dishonor others, it is not self-seeking, it is not easily angered, it keeps no record of wrongs. Love does not delight in evil but rejoices with the truth. It always protects, always trusts, always hopes, always perseveres. Love never fails.

1 CORINTHIANS 13:4–8 NIV

ON HATING YOURSELF AND WHY YOU CAN BE VULNERABLE TO JESUS

LAST NIGHT WASN'T MY BEST NIGHT. THE house was a royal wreck, *again*. Seems like it's always a royal wreck, again, and I muttered under my breath we were all slobs, but I believed it was mostly my own fault. If I could be more organized. If I could quit wasting so much time. *If I could do better and be better.* I had a whole list of reasons starting with *If I could ...* It's amazing how quick a girl can wear herself out by focusing on how much she doesn't measure up.

Brent had lovingly offered to help me clean up the house, but instead of picking up one more sock or another toy, I gave up

and retreated to the bed and called it quits. The only problem was the kids were still wide awake and enthusiastic. So he brushed their teeth and tucked them in while I yelled from the covers my goodnights and "I'll see you folks tomorrow!" I desperately hoped things would look a little less bleak the next morning.

Then I lay there and sort of pined away. Because I had done some things earlier that made me feel dumb. So I told myself some mean things. *You're an idiot. You're a stupid idiot. Everyone knows you are. Idiot, that's you.* For some reason I thought it would help because I had felt it, therefore it must be true. And I wasn't going to talk myself out of my slump. I was going to close my eyes and block it out with sleep in hopes it would all go away.

But Brent came. He curled up next to me and pulled me close and gently asked me to please talk to him. I wasn't going to. There was no way I was going to tell him what I was thinking. But he was so kind and he did want to know, so I slowly but surely spilled it out. There was the house stuff and the "I'm a stupid idiot" stuff, and before I knew it, I was telling him about ten other things I didn't even know were right there, crammed down in my complicated heart. And the whole time Brent didn't try to fix my problems, nor would he agree with my ill assessment of myself or condone my demeaning talk. He listened and spoke some tender truth where he could, but mostly he nodded and said, "Yeah, I feel like that sometimes, too . . . but it's not true."

Afterward I felt the sweetest peace because there was all this release. I looked at Brent and thought he was surely never more like Jesus than when he was holding me tight and loving all my insides, ugly and messed up as they were.

Because isn't Jesus this way? At least, He *desires* to be. Jesus is a Lover and He wants to draw us close, but we've got to open up to Him. We're like this little green leaf and Christ is like the sun. He shines the warmth of His love on us, and our job is to open wide toward Him. We've got to tell Him all our troubles and spill out all our angst and be as honest as can be. Jesus wants to whisper tender truth. But how will we hear His voice unless we're vulnerable to Him?

It's when we let down the walls and speak the ugly out loud in the dark that we find a Lover who doesn't loathe our raw and real and won't confirm all our self-condemnation. Instead, He woos us to Himself and washes away all the fear of failing. His love swallows up our hate. He sends sweet mercies running at the first blush of each new day.

> *The steadfast love of the Lord never ceases;*
> *his mercies never come to an end;*
> *they are new every morning;*
> *great is your faithfulness.*

LAMENTATIONS 3:22–23

> *There is therefore now no condemnation for those who are in Christ Jesus.*

ROMANS 8:1

ON FINDING GOD
IN A BROKEN WORLD

DEAR CHILDREN,

This momma of yours sometimes lies awake at night worrying about the world and about you and how you'll grow up here. There are these moments when I've read the latest headline on the news that I want to lock the doors and all the evil out and try my best to protect you from everything wicked and wild.

I wish you could only know about blazing sunsets and fishing ponds and old barns down dirt roads and kitties and good people that call you friends and a society that's safe to live in. But things are broken here, and there's some things I need to tell you to keep you soul-safe. I want the light in your heart to stay on when the world around you gets dark.

There's a God who is good, who does love you and who's got this whole world in His hands. But there will be days when it won't feel that way. You'll look around and sit numb from the pointlessness of it all and grasp for answers, knowing full well sometimes there are things that happen here you will not understand.

Keep praying to the God I've told you about. Because when we pray, we reach out and grab hold of Someone real but who can't be seen. There will be aching nights when you will struggle along, feeling around in the dark, searching for some notion of grace in this fallen world. And I want you to hear me—God is *here*. Right here. And when you run hard after Him, determined to find Him with a little speck of faith, He will show up. Every once in a while you'll be able to feel Him— the warmth of His light-bearing face.

I know, my loves, you'll have your doubts. The voices around you and sometimes in you will try to reason God away. Clouds of unbelief will hide from you what's there. Cynicism will come looking for you, to hunt you down. You'll have to do war, my loves. You'll need to turn around and look at that sneering unbelief in the face and scream the truth you've got tucked down deep in your heart. You'll have to kick doubt to the curb, babes, or it will cling to you.

Remember it's sin, not God, that broke this whole place. The ground groans. Stars catapult in revolt and trees travail like a woman in labor pain, bent over and gasping for her next breath. Creation reels for all that's been lost and waits with this eager longing to be set free and restored to her rhythm of rest once again (Rom. 8:19–24).

You'll wonder why you're here. Just keep running to your Maker and He'll whisper it to you again, because it bears repeating. That you are light and couriers of His love, and this is how He chooses to help the world—through your actual hands. Your very feet. He'll shine out through your eyes and His joy will show up in your cheeks and in your smile. You, His kingdom children, will demonstrate to the world a different way.

And when you're afraid about your life, remember God knows the number of your days (Ps. 139:16). He's with you in every single one of them. Don't forget, you must never forget, there is a forever after this. One day light will split through all these cracks and God's righteous kingdom will reign. *Forever*. There will be no more sickness or dying, and all that's sad will come to an end. You'll hear it then—how the mountains will shout for the everlasting joy being born, the thorns in the thickets will no longer grow, and all the trees in the field will clap their hands (Isa. 55:12–13).

So long as I've got this breath in my lungs, I'll remind you of these things. And I'll help you see that though the world is broken, still it's good. There's beauty here and God-glory all around. I'll take you by the hand and we'll go hunting. We won't stop looking until we find Him here. Together we'll trace the outlines of His ways.

As long as you're here with me, I'll keep getting up and stumbling through the dark to check on you while you're fast asleep. And even when you're grown and gone, I'll still carry you around in my heart and chase you with my prayers. You'll always have your momma's prayers, my loves. Tonight I'm praying for your peace.

The night is nearly over; the day is almost here.
ROMANS 13:12 NIV

Here's another way to put it: You're here to be light, bringing out the God-colors in the world. God is not a secret to be kept. We're going public with this, as public as a city on a hill. If I make you light-bearers, you don't think I'm going to hide you under a bucket, do you? I'm putting you on a light stand. Now that I've put you there on a hilltop, on a light stand—shine! Keep open house; be generous with your lives. By opening up to others, you'll prompt people to open up with God, this generous Father in heaven.

MATTHEW 5:14–16 THE MESSAGE

You will seek me and find me when you seek me with all your heart. I will be found by you.

JEREMIAH 29:13–14 NIV

A PRAYER OF BLESSING—
TO THE READER

DEAR ONE,

I hope by the time you've gotten here, to the end, you've caught a glimpse, in some way, of the God of glory who's always been. The One who breathed and stars came out. Who spoke and the moon woke up to shine. The One who knit you together when you were in your momma's tummy and held you in His heart long before time as we know it began.

And I hope you've met with Him here—this God whose face is so full of glory it always shines. I've prayed for you. Because I want you to believe in Him and to know Him. And though your heart may be jaded and your fears left you tempest-tossed, I want you to trust Him, to know down deep in your gut that this One with the countenance all radiant bright turns toward *you* and seeks to bless you. And if you would have Him, He would cup your cheeks in His nail-scarred hands, look deep in your eyes, and whisper words tender and true.

So this I ask of Him, and for you:

May the Lord bless you and keep you, bringing what's truly good into your life.

May He build around you His safekeeping. May the blood of Christ wash you white as snow and the Spirit of Jesus hem you in, above and beneath you, behind and before you. May He be your shield and your exceedingly great reward.

May the Lord be gracious to you, His smile be upon you, His love always moving toward you. And may you know He is *for* you.

The Lord lift up His countenance upon you, look right your way and *shine*. May He open the eyes of your heart so you will recognize, time and time again, all the ways He shows up throughout your day.

And may He give you peace: the kind that defies all logic and human understanding. May He, who makes everything come together for good, come and settle you down, calm your spirit, make you whole.

And since peace comes from His Presence, may you live your life increasingly mindful of the One who formed you and knows you. Deep down knows and absolutely loves you. May you walk each moment ever before the God with the shining face.

> *The Lord bless you and keep you;*
> *the Lord make his face to shine upon you*
> *and be gracious to you;*
> *the Lord lift up his countenance upon you*
> *and give you peace.*
>
> NUMBERS 6:24–26

Can you see it now?

How there's *glory* in the grime?

Yes, even there

at the kitchen sink.

MAGGIE PAULUS is a beauty seeker who looks for God in each day He has given her. She lives in Michigan with her bearded husband, three rambunctious kids, and one cat. When she is not capturing life in words and photos, you'll find her digging in the dirt, eating chocolate, and garage sale-ing with her family.

You can connect with Maggie online at MaggiePaulus.com or find her on Twitter @MaggiePaulus.

ACKNOWLEDGMENTS

Firstly, I want to thank Rene'. Rene' Hanebutt, affectionately known in my house as Naner.

For without her there would be no book. I remember the day she stood on the staircase of the office at work and told me that she was going to make me an author. And she did. Not many people have a friend like that. A friend who sees something in you that you don't even recognize in yourself, and who decides to carry that something around in their heart and then invest their life into making a shining dream become reality. Thank you, Naner. You're like this book's momma. And you've been a good momma.

And thank you to Moody Publishers for giving this a chance. Paul Santhouse, for your kindness. Holly Kisley, for that initial meeting where you encouraged me that this book didn't have to have chapters. And that it could even have pictures! You were a breath of fresh air to this girl who doesn't think in a straight line, but in a wiggle. Thank you, Bailey Utecht, for your beautiful editing abilities and for making this better. And Pam Pugh, for coming alongside during the last leg and bringing this all together.

Also, I want to thank my friends Deb and Victoria. These are the friends I meet with nearly once a week, to pray for ourselves and our families and for the world. They've prayed for these words. So thank you, girls. You've helped shape who I am.

And to my family, Ma and Pa. Alan, Ginny, David. Thank you for being a family to me. For all the forgiving and forbearing. For all the praying and sticking together. Even in the hard. I love you each, deep.

Also, I want to thank my beautiful farmin' in-laws who have helped me, by spending time with these grandkids of theirs, so I could write. Mary, thank you especially for your servant's heart.

And thank you, Brent. For helping me carve out time to write. For helping me to process life. For praying for me when I was scared. And for loving me when I was unlovely. I'm so glad I get to share this life with you.

And lastly, I want to thank my God. The Maker of me. *Yahweh*, the God who gives me all my breaths. Thank You for giving me words and for meeting with me here. For showing me Your glory and for being my Home. This is for You, Jesus. Please take these words, send them out into the wide world and use them to help and heal. Take this little thing that I've got and rescue Your kids. Bring them into Your Kingdom, Lord. Amen.

MADE FOR MORE

978-0-8024-1032-0

Is your identity based on a role? Is it linked to a relationship? Do your achievements influence how you view yourself? What does your family say about you? Who are you as a woman?

Honestly, these are not the right questions. The real question is, who are you as a person created in God's image? Until we see our identity in His, we're settling for seconds. And we were made for so much more …

Also available as an ebook

MOODY
PUBLISHERS

PACKING LIGHT

When I was in college, I figured my life would come together around graduation. I'd meet a guy; we'd plan a beautiful wedding and buy a nice house—not necessarily with a picket fence, but with whatever kind of fence we wanted. I might work, or I might not, but whatever we decided, I would be happy. I got out of college and my life didn't look like that. Just when I had given up all hope of finding the "life I'd always dreamed about," I decided to take a trip to all fifty states… because when you go on a trip, you can't take your baggage. What I found was that "packing light" wasn't as easy as I thought it was

Also available as an ebook

MOODY
PUBLISHERS

www.MoodyPublishers.com

JAVA WITH JULI

Brewing rich conversations, delivering bold truth.

Pour yourself a cup of coffee and enjoy **Java with Juli**, a new podcast by host and clinical psychologist Dr. Juli Slattery. From the cozy setting of a coffee shop, Juli offers a woman's perspective on intimacy and converses with guests about the challenges of being a contemporary Christian woman.

www.moodyradio.org/javawithjuli

MOODYRADIO

Where you turn. For life.